WORD MAGIC

WORD MAGIC

How to Encourage Children to Write and Speak Creatively

Charleen Whisnant and Jo Hassett

Doubleday & Company, Inc., Garden City, New York
1974

372.6
W576w

Library of Congress Cataloging in Publication Data
Whisnant, Charleen.
    Word magic.
    1. Language arts (Primary)   I. Hassett, Jo, joint
author.   II. Title.
LB1528.W47   1974   372.6
Library of Congress Catalog Number 73–83683
ISBN 0-385-06823-9
ISBN 0-385-06832-8 (pbk.)

For our children,
Ena, Karen, Marjorie, and Thomas
and the children who wrote the poems

Acknowledgments

We are indebted to the following poet-teachers who shared their ideas and gave support: Ardis Kimzey, Heather Ross Miller, Campbell Reeves, Stanley Burns, Carolyn Kizer, Paul Newman, Ruth Lisa Schlecter, Julie Suk, Maria Ingram, Jim Thompson, Audrey Wall, Marion Cannon, and Dr. Emerson Johnson.

We would like to acknowledge the following schools in whose classrooms most of the poetry for this book was written: Charlotte Country Day School, Robert Kennedy Junior High School, Gastonia Central Elementary School, Thomasville Colonial Drive School, Edenton Ernest A. Swain Elementary School, Marion McDowell High School, Charlotte Beverly Woods School, Charlotte First Ward School, Charlotte Carmel Junior High School, Rockford Illinois Keith Country Day School.

We thank the North Carolina Department of Public Instruction for permission to reprint poems from their Poets in the Schools Anthology, *All I Have for Tenderness Is Words*.

Contents

1. Creative Language

A young girl remarked to her adult companion, "I wish I were dumb! It is easier to be happy if you are dumb!" Her friend answered quickly and with obvious annoyance, "You don't mean that. You are already dumb if that is what you want to be." That was the end of the conversation. An opportunity for creative listening, talking, and human relationship had been lost. The child was petulant over sensing her own unrealized possibilities and if she had been encouraged to explore and explain her feelings, she might have discovered that her restlessness is typical of any creative searching.

This book is about creative listening, talking, reading, and writing. It is about the fulfillment of human potential through the articulation of bad or beautiful feelings, of questions, of dangerous or poetic thoughts. It is about the enrichment of our perceptions and relationships through creative expression. It is about the frustration and waste of unfulfilled expression.

The encouragement of creativity is critical to life. The human mind has already conceived of human demise but has yet to creatively control human continuance. In the classroom where works of art and science are dissected, students have been directed to analyze creativity more often than they have been free to practice it.

Creativity in its best sense, the imagining of solutions to problems, belongs to all of us. To be human is to be creative. Sorting through our thoughts by expressing our feelings in language is natural and easy for us as children, but as we are buffeted with more and more information, as life grows complex, it seems risky to respond in language. Verbalization, however, is necessary to the understanding of our experience. Language enables us to penetrate ourselves, to locate and discover feelings that we have forgotten but which continue to direct our behavior.

Verbalization is an important defense against anxiety. It gives us a feeling of being alive, of being worth something, of affecting the inevitable unwinding of our lives, of affecting the lives of others, of having some influence over environment and fate.

Our experience as human beings is essentially mysterious and unfathomable. Language works as a defense against a sense of sterility, an overwhelming perception of separation and solitude. Creative language uses more than the mind, uses also emotion, and therefore becomes a more total interchange between more total people. Language makes relationships with others possible; it affects the quality of those relationships; it is fulfilling beyond the mere sharing of information. The expression of our feelings in language produces a heightened awareness of oneself and of others.

Language also has power over our experience. Verbalizing works like magic to prevent the unique from becoming commonplace. It keeps our commitments fresh. It prevents our taking life for granted. It satisfies a basic human impulse to cherish and preserve, to honor those things that we love.

This book suggests that we utilize these powers of creative language more fully by considering its several opportunities as creative listening, reading, talking, and writing. Our schools seem to have emphasized reading and writing to the disadvantage of creative explorations of talking and listening. In this book, we have tried to gather exercises for the stimulation of creativity in each of these areas where articulation is important and can be an adventure.

2. An Environment for Creative Language

The creativity evident in the art work of children reflects their wonder about life. Children wonder about everything. They are able to see the everlasting newness, the deep down freshness of things. To be wondering about life always is to lead an inspired life, and the preservation of this sense of wonder is necessary to continued creativity. This quality seems ironically to lessen as children are exposed to education. It would seem that adults are trying to take the mystery out of life, to communicate along with knowledge a matter of fact attitude toward knowledge.

Educators and parents comment on the lessening of inspiration and freedom in the expressions of children as they progress through school. In order to prevent this loss of imagination in our children, we need to consider the sort of environment which would sustain their basic creative ability.

Freedom, stimulation, and response are necessary to the child so that he may continue to express himself creatively and joyfully. Imagination is free-ranging, seemingly irrational thought, and freedom is critical to its existence. It is frequently stifled for the sake of teaching discipline. Nonschematic free association in the minds of our children does not seem productive to us and is seldom encouraged.

As parents and educators we believe that it is important to train and correct our children for accuracy in a world that demands it. We continually exercise our young at home and at school with questions like, "Is that what you really mean? What actually happened? Is that right? What is the point?" to the exclusion of exercises and attitudes that would sustain their creativity such as, "Talk about it some more. How might things have been different? How did you feel? Is that all of it? Add on, include, imagine more. Think freely, associate, include mystery."

One of the problems of course is that we adults are always busy. At home where parents feel it is necessary to make a point to their children and have it accepted or at school where the teacher has a lesson plan to be accomplished, the child becomes a hindrance if he persists in creative random thinking, verbalization which seems to the controlling adult to be tangential.

The need to hurry is inhibiting to any creativity. Speculation takes time, thrives on leisure. In the process of speculation or creative expression, exploration, risks, and errors should be accepted and encouraged. A child who is trying to express his feelings and thoughts should hear from a creative listener, "Yes, yes, I almost understand, go on." Realizing that nothing, no experience or feeling is ever completely or adequately expressed in language eases the frustration of both listener and talker, gives freedom to reader and writer. An understanding that uncertainty and groping are inevitable in creative and honest expression produces paradoxically a sense of security and certainty in the use of language.

The attitude of expecting to gamble, of expecting ineptitudes, even inaccuracy, in articulate gropings makes it possible to stumble across spontaneous insights and deeper communications. Freedom and experimentation in language are necessary in any environment that would sustain creative language use. They will produce an open mouth and prevent a closing mind, circumstances sometimes tedious to adults but always desirable for the sake of creative children.

3. Exercises in Language for the Preschool Child

Creative listening is an important ingredient in language environment. It requires time, patience, and a real interest in the developing child. Many adults drift into believing that their own ideas are much more significant and deserving of articulation than any which the child might express. But an environment which will sustain and nurture creative expression requires mutual sharing, equal time in endless conversations. The most significant conversations to the child are probably the ones that he instigates. It is when he wants to ask or share that he is most stimulated to search for ways to express himself. It is then that he will use his imagination extensively to put feelings and thoughts into words. When parents and teachers respond attentively and enthusiastically to these language efforts, they contribute significantly to creative growth.

Creative listening to a child's attempts to express himself is necessary to his continued attempt and success in communication with others. The communication of his feelings and thoughts is also critical to any assistance we might give the child, any diagnosis of his needs or guidance in his development. Unfortunately a child's inability to communicate becomes most obvious when he stops, when he withdraws emotionally or intellectually from us. When a child has lost joy and faith in language he turns to other means of establishing relationships which may be destructive to his health or psyche. It is then that language is critical as therapy, that we must restore to the child the expression of himself and communication with others through creative listening.

Faith in the importance of communication is established early in the child's life and is closely related to the pleasure that language gives him, pleasure that is most possible if he has a creative listener available. A concerned and caring adult will recognize and stimulate opportunity for listening and verbalization throughout the child's development. From the earliest years when a child at solitary play talks to himself, opportunities will occur. These early "out loud" monologues will consist of repetitions and interpretations of language and ideas that the child has overheard. In the restructuring of these the child is using his creative language power and he will profit throughout his growth if he learns that adults value and encourage such attempts. He can learn in preschool years that his curiosity is interesting, that discussion can be helpful and occur at any time, that wonder and investigation are pleasures which can be shared in language throughout his life.

The very young child, in the course of normal development, acquires enough language to become fluent. One day the child seems to have become a perpetual talker. Parents who are not prepared for this might find themselves overcome, and they might begin to establish a defense mechanism of child deafness which is not unlike a situation all of us have seen in children who develop "parent deafness" in order to defend themselves against parents who are continually evaluating them and directing their thoughts and acts. This lack of creative listening on the part of either parents or children is a condition dangerous to the development of creativity and is absolutely destructive of creative relationships.

CREATIVE TALKING

As the young child begins to talk he learns that language works, that it can make things happen. As he learns that people respond to language signals, he begins to experiment with a wider vocabulary and its effects. Interest in a child's invented expressions and explanations when he misinterprets words promotes an ever-widening vocabulary. When the child gets to school he will probably engage in an exercise in which he is asked to use new words in a sentence. It is good to do this before the child gets to school and parents might expand the game creatively by asking for new words to be used in an idea as well as in a sentence. Encourage the child to imagine some situation in which they would need that new word; ask them to describe the circumstance and use the word.

Another game of enjoying words consists of naming things which are new or unfamiliar: people on the bus or animals seen at the zoo or the circus might be called "Hector," or "Friendly Face," or "tonoimatachumaphala." A game to be played with young children while traveling might be finding verbs, adverbs, and adjectives to describe what they see. The sunlit cows might be dreaming or the hungry bulldozer chewing the dirt. It is also fun to talk imaginatively about common things, the lazy houseplants or the snoring refrigerator. Sensitive adults realize that the child is not only building vocabulary, the vocabulary is shaping the child's awareness and creativity.

Conversations with preschool children will enable them to practice their vocabulary, will improve speaking and listening skills, and will help with written language later. These conversations can of course occur at any time on any subject but they are especially valuable to creativity when they are related to activities.

When the child is at play, ask him about what he is doing. When parents are working at home they can encourage the child to help or imitate. Tell the child what you are doing. Tell him the names of the tools or utensils you are using. Let him use your materials or provide him with a toy set for his exploratory activities and your conversations about them. Manipulation is basic to creative activity and is a precursor of discovery and invention. Connecting language to manipulative and exploratory experience augments the creative potential of the activities as well as the language.

Another activity which lends itself to creative conversations with young children is drawing. Children love to make pictures and to talk about them. You might speculate with the child about the names of the people in the picture, what they are doing, what they have just done, and what they might do next. Discuss the families of the people in the picture, things they like to do and things they don't like to do. The young child is rehearsing life in his drawing and in his creative talk. Encourage him. Ask him questions about his drawing or painting. Accept his explanations and definitions of what he is doing and what it means to him. Remember that adverse criticism is destructive of joy in creative activities. It is better that purple faces or any other pictorialization which seems unusual to you be accepted openly and with special interest. Unusual approaches are fundamental to creativity.

If the young child has had pleasant experiences in conversation with adults, he will be eager to have conversation with his playmates. Make maximum creativity possible in these conversations by providing stimulating materials such as large cardboard boxes that can be imagined as boats, houses, or space ships. Provide dress-up clothes and flexible props. If imagination and language need some stimulation you might suggest that they play at being somebody else, that they act out stories with which they are familiar, or that they make up and act out their own stories. Puppets are also conducive to creative language use and a good excuse for children to engage in that grand activity of "putting on a show."

Storytelling is an exercise in creative talking that can begin when a child is very young and can develop into significant sharing and creativity between parent and child. Telling a story is different from reading one. There is a different language quality in the told story, a different relationship between the storyteller and the listener than exists between the story reader and the listener. When the child looks at the speaker, he listens and understands better. The expression on the face of the storyteller is an important dimension of the experience. The child reads the storyteller's face and perceives there the excitement, suspense, mystery, fun, nonsense, or whatever the words convey. The expression of the storyteller helps the child interpret the meaning of the words and understand what a great variety of feeling language can express.

It is a great pleasure to remember and tell stories that you learned as a child, but do not limit yourself to known stories. Try making up stories. Children learn to be creative by observing creative activity. They love to hear stories about their parents' childhood. Or make up stories with the child as a character. Tell about the things he does. Try telling about things you wish he would do. Make up stories in which you do wildly wonderful things together.

CREATIVE READING

It is never too soon to start using books with children. The loving act of holding a small child, turning pages in a book, and talking about the pictures makes a significant emotional connection between language and pleasure. Naming the animals and objects in the pictures develops vocabulary. As the child's understanding grows, you can tell stories about the pictures. Let him tell you stories about them. Ask him questions to get him started. What might you both be doing if you were in the picture? You start a story about the picture and ask the child to finish it.

Continue reading books to children even after they begin school, even after they learn to read for themselves. They will be refreshed and encouraged by an exposure to the books that they can someday read for themselves. As they learn to read you might enjoy reading favorite books together, taking turns with the pages. You might make up new adventures for characters in the stories. Perhaps you can write these stories down. The child can dictate them and illustrate them. These efforts can easily be made into books with staples or commercial binders. Such booklets made out of the child's own creativity will be so loved and partially memorized that they will be a significant step in his learning to read.

4. The School Age Child

When the child goes to school he enjoys new opportunities for language stimulation and response but suffers an inevitable loss of freedom. Difficulty with the mechanics of writing, spelling, and grammar, and the pressure to do acceptable work, may inhibit his creative expression and his honesty. The joy he had in language as a talker may be displaced by frustration as he struggles to read and write. It is important that language exercises are not confined to these two skills, that the skills of reading and writing are not considered knowledge itself. All students need to continue to enjoy and refine their language skills through oral exercises. Talking is the most effective way for people of any age to learn to use a language for thinking and communicating. At elementary school levels it would be effective to teach logic and sustain creativity through much more talking and less writing. Children love the opportunity for self-expression but it is inhibited by the difficulties we impose on it through writing or lack of opportunity to talk creatively.

Exercises in creative talk remind us that education can be fun, that language can be used as a means to understand experience, that logic is useful in developing ideas and in communicating them to another person. Here are a few ideas for such exercises that can be used between parents and children, at school, in any group as games or enrichment experiences.

A word game for very young children involves guessing what the game leader sees from a description given by the leader. "I see something in the room that is shiny and silver. What is it called?" (the door knob) "I see something that would feel warm to the touch." Two different answers (the light bulb or a person) would teach that more complete description is needed, that communication requires detail.

Creative talk, like creative writing, is more exciting and fruitful when it grows out of mutual and immediate experience. Try spraying the room with scented air freshener. Have everyone close his eyes in order to concentrate on the experience of smell. Ask them to contribute ideas about what the smell reminds them of and this can evolve into talking a collaboration poem about smell, or into individuals talking their own paragraphs about smell. This is a good way to teach that a paragraph is a group of ideas about one aspect of a topic. All the ideas about good smells would be in one paragraph and the ideas about bad smells might come in a following paragraph. This exercise can be changed or enlarged by the sharing of taste, a piece of candy for everyone or an apple, by listening to a piece of music. Exciting sessions have evolved when children were exposed simultaneously to a good smell, a good taste, music, swatches of velvet to feel, and were then asked to write or talk a paragraph describing "The World of Perfect Pleasure." What would we eat, drink, see in such a world? What sensations would be left out of such a world?

A DIALOG ABOUT THE PERFECT WORLD

If the world were perfect
We would eat perfect food.
It would taste like hamburgers
    with mustard and pickle.

We would have perfect water,
    fresh as the mountain water.
We would have perfect clothes
    colored silver.
We would have perfect houses,
    big and painted orange.
There would be no fighting
    we wouldn't need any policemen.
We could go around the world.
We wouldn't have to go to school.
We wouldn't have to wash our clothes
Or patch our blue jeans.

Doug and Ronnie, *age 9*

There are many simple games that can be played in the class-room to give impetus to creative thought and talk. One of the simplest is to bring many different kinds of hats into the room. Distribute the policeman's hat, the fireman's hat, the baker's, the business hat, an assortment of ladies' hats, and have the children talk like the person who would wear such a hat. Each character can imagine a personality that suits his hat and many combinations and dialogues can evolve in this game. If the furniture can be cleared away, the game of "Sling the Statue," which most children know, can make an interesting starting point for talk about what statues can commemorate, where they can be located, how long they last, and what it would feel like to be a statue.

There are several games to the rhythms of snapping fingers or clapping hands. These games can be used imaginatively to stimulate interest and play with language. In one such game children sit in a circle and establish the rhythm of slapping their own knees twice and then snapping fingers of first one hand and then the other in a rhythm of one/two, three/four. Once the rhythm is established, talk can be added, a story told one by one around the circle, each child adding a sentence without breaking the rhythm. Rhyming often occurs in this exercise and adds to the fun. Such an exercise might produce:

I am a man
I live down town
I wear green clothes
I have black toes
I eat fat worms
I skate all day
I snore at night
Beside my dog
Who keeps me warm

Another game that points up the variety of language and of individual differences in observation is called "Word Images." The teacher, poet, or one of the students suggests a simple word like dog or house, or running. Everyone in the room then makes a mental picture of what the word suggests to them. The sharing of these detailed responses is interesting and could evolve into a collaboration poem.

"Talking Portraits" is another language game which can be an experience in the different approaches that individuals can have in their perception of another person. Ask each person to choose someone in the room, study that person for a while, and then make in words a portrait of that person. If various means of description are discussed beforehand, this exercise will not deteriorate into mere repetition of approach. Suggest individuality of portraiture by reminding that we use our senses in perceiving people, and that we make comparisons to other people. It might also be enriching to show famous portraits such as the Mona Lisa, Van Gogh's self-portrait, Picasso's "Girl at the Mirror" and to discuss the detail and emphasis that painters choose in trying to make a true re-creation of personality.

Trips are another useful experience to stimulate creative talking. They need not be important trips; a walk through the halls of school will do if you talk about it beforehand, speculate about the kinds of things you might observe, and compare perceptions afterward. Talk, talk, talk, encourage imagination, logic, awareness.

Play newscaster. The teacher can tell about the trip as though she were a newscaster. The children can do the same. This is a fine opportunity for pointing out the differences in colloquial speech, dialects, and standard English. There need never be a suggestion that the newscaster's speech is right and some other is wrong, but rather that it is different. Placing value judgments on one form of expression as compared to another form is largely an adult concern. The children do not think about differences in expression that way. One speech is used at home, one at school, and we use them appropriately.

Other exercises in creative talking include: giving directions, explaining feelings, persuading people, and telling stories. Ask each child to think about something he knows how to do and could explain to others so that they could also do it. Good topics might include baking a cake, inventing a machine, building a model airplane, damming a creek, traveling to another part of the city. Explain that this is an exercise in logic and sequence, and that the listeners will discuss whether or not they could actually follow the given directions.

EXPLAINING THE TELEPORTER

I'd like to invent a teleporter. It would be made up of two glass capsules, some wires, a few buttons, and a few accessories. You would send one of the glass capsules to your Great Aunt Agnes in New York (or anywhere else for that matter). Then your Great Aunt Agnes (or whoever you sent the capsule to) would hook the wire to the top of the capsule and then she would call you on the phone while you were at home (or wherever you were) and tell you that the wire was hooked. Then you would hook your end of the wire to the top of the capsule and step inside. Then WHAM, by superelectrical process which until now was unknown to man, you would shrink to the size of a molecule and fly through the wire at twice the speed of light and you would land in the other capsule at your Great Aunt Agnes' house (or wherever the other capsule was) and regain your normal size.

John Holder, *age 11*

Explain feelings, talk about how it feels to be happy, sad, embarrassed, or try this experiment if you have some experience or interest in creative dramatics. Ask the children to stand up and close their eyes. Ask them to pretend they are growing larger and larger, and as they grow to stretch their arms, to concentrate on growing larger. When they have stretched themselves into as large a space as possible, ask them to think about shrinking very slowly and to continue thinking about shrinking, using their bodies to help them until they are curled tightly on the floor. After this experience, ask each of them to talk about how it felt to concentrate, to grow, to shrink.

HOW I FEEL

When I hear the thunder I think of the boomings of God. The rain comes down so evenly, just as three follows two. I think of the darkness and gloominess of the heavens. When I'm walking by myself I think that I am lonely. When I get home I feel more safe.

Curtis Brownell, *age 11*

Persuasion is a challenge and keeps its focus on language best if emotional topics are avoided. The advantages of one automobile over another, the best pet, the best place to live are all good topics. Listeners to the argument are involved by discussing the strength and persuasiveness of what they hear.

A PET CAN BE A FRIEND

I think you should try to treat animals like your best friend. I try. I can't always do it. It takes love. Once a dog on a trip got lost hundreds of miles from his home. In a period of six months that dog searched and searched until he found his home. People saw him in six states and that dog must have gone about 25,000 miles. When you are in your bed at night do you ever get scared? Well, if you gave that dog love, he would stay and watch you in your sleep.

Nolan Mills, *age 10*

The telling of stories is a delight to everyone. An exercise that can both be fun and increase the child's ability to improve his English is the opportunity to act out stories that have been read to him. The very young child will enjoy a story like "The Three Bears," while older children might prefer stories and characters out of their history books or newspapers.

Other good ideas for talked stories include the "built-on" story in which teacher, parent, or children alternately add incidents in a narrative from surroundings familiar to life or shared literary experience. If the story is very dramatic and the idea of acquiring an adult's vocabulary is made a part of the game, then the growth of language keeps pace with imagination.

The "Point of View" story game relates clear thinking to creativity. Take one incident and have people tell about it from different points of view. If you use stories with which the children are already familiar, this exercise can be rich in the potential for making judgments about how one character can see an incident in a different way than another character.

Two Talked Stories:

THE GOOD LIFE

If I were going to have a good life, I would buy an elephant. That would make me happy and I would never be sad. I would ride my elephant every day. I would feed him very well and then one day I would enter him in the circus. They would pay me well and after that I would marry a famous ballet dancer. We would be rich and we would have five children. Then one day I would buy my children an elephant. They would hug me and they would love me always.

Derrick Joyner, *age 8*

A CHRISTMAS STORY

It was three days until Christmas and everyone was happy except Fred, the mouse that lived in our house. He lived alone because his father had died in a trap and his mother ate poison. Fred is a pretty mouse with fur of silver, but that did not make his situation any better. One of his problems, besides danger, was that he never got any presents. He thought about this for two days and he finally decided not to eat the people's cheese. Instead he left them some of his cheese. Christmas morning he found a whole pound of cheese and the true meaning of Christmas. Give a little, take a little.

Rick Gaylord, *age 10*

A Built-On Story:

THE WITCH

The witch house is at the bus stop
    over near the gate.
The witch house is black and brown.
It is a scary house made out of bricks.
It's got a big pot outside that the witch
    cooks brew in.

The witch looks like a woman and she lives
    in the house with her friends.
She's got a lot of beds and a stove.
She has a bat and an alligator and a
    black cat, a brown dog, and a magic broom.
She flies on the magic broom.
She's got a pot with some stew in it
    and she stirs it with a broom.
There are spider webs in the house.
One day I knocked on her door
    and she let me in.
She wanted to get me and put me on a broom.
I heard some of her magic stuff cooking.
I looked, and it was red.
There were sheep and snakes in the house.
The witch had a cat on her back.
She wanted me to sleep with her cat.
The cat flew on her broom.
She gave me some chocolate cake and she
    was nice to me.
She gave me some candy.
She bought another house, and she got very rich,
    and she got rid of that cat.

        Grade 1

IDEAS FOR WRITING PROSE

Exercise in creative talking should be continued and continually encouraged. The skill of writing prose grows simultaneously and will be easier if the student has understood talking as a skill. The exercise in giving directions as conversation is also a good assignment in writing prose. This kind of writing is called "expository writing" at the upper grade levels but is better understood at lower grade levels when termed "explanatory writing." When encouraging the writing of prose, you might well begin with explanatory writing and such exercises as, "Tell about yourself," "explain your hobby," "describe a place," or "give logical directions about how to make something or get somewhere."

THE BEST BEDROOM

The Governor's Mansion at Williamsburg has a master bedroom that takes up almost half of the third floor. The washstand is made of silver and the washbasin of brass. The dresser has secret slots and drawers for valuables since there were no safes in those days. There is a large closet in the bedroom that has secret drawers for expensive furs. The bedroom has a balcony made of wire that looks like a lace veil. From the balcony you can see a stream that sparkles like the rainbow in the sunshine. Branches of the trees cross overhead like an upsidedown green lace cup.

Marla Shapiro, *age 10*

Another assignment in prose that often captures the imagination of children is writing letters. Ask them to write a letter to a famous person, someone in history they admire, someone they do not anticipate meeting but with whom they would like to have a communication, someone to whom they have something special to communicate. Children have written moving letters to the dogcatcher, the President of the United States, to parents expressing feelings that the child had not been given opportunity to explain.

Dear Neal Armstrong,

How did it feel when you stepped on the moon?

Was it squishy? Was it hard? Was it hot or cold? Was it bouncy? I wish I could find out for myself.

> Sincerely,
> John Taylor, *age 12*

Dear People From Outer Space:

I saw a film that showed things people could not have done or known without some very intelligent people telling or directing. They said you were here long ago. I think you were. If you helped people in the past and you are friendly, will you help us now?

> Your friend,
> Allen Burt, *age 13*

P.S.   Please show your intentions are friendly because some people here shoot before they think.

Dear Grandmother,

I wish I could have known you before you died. Why did you die right before I was born? There is a picture of you in our living room with your husband. I hope you are both happy. Can you see me or hear me? Do you know what I am doing? Please write me and tell me about yourself and your life.

> Love,
> Your granddaughter Margaret

P.S.   If possible, how about a visit?

> Margaret Storrs, *age 12*

Imitation of an author's style is fun and instructive. Read from a writer with a distinctive style. Kipling does well as an example for younger children; Vachel Lindsay's poems, Stephen Crane's short surrealistic poems, Walt Whitman's laundry lists of celebration, or Hemingway's style for older children. Ask the students to try to write in the style of this author. An imitation of subject matter is inevitable in this exercise and it would be a help to discuss in advance of the actual exercise several topics that the individual authors might have found attractive, topics that children might use.

If you are interested in exercises in narrative, story seeds are effective. The story seed can be taken from a picture, from a situation suggested by the teacher or the students, an idea in the newspaper, or a short story. The beginnings should be kept simple and lively and the story can be finished by the group sharing together or by the children individually. Try some of the following starters for stories: Here is a photograph of a man and a woman in a canoe. They see a big rock ahead. Finish the story. Here is a photograph of the Governor's Mansion. Tell a story about it. Or from O. Henry: A boy and girl who are very much in love have no money to buy one another a Christmas gift. What can they do? ("Gift of the Magi") When the children have made up their own story, it is fun and instructive to show where the idea came from and how the original author finished the story.

Other good assignments for writing stories are telling the further adventures of a favorite storybook character. Winnie the Pooh, Black Beauty, Gulliver, or Tom Sawyer are examples of characters that work well.

Provocative titles that are provided by parents, teachers, or imagined by the students themselves are engaging story starters. "The Forgotten Toy," "The Imaginary Friend," "My Most Vivid Memory" might lead into all sorts of inspiring possibilities.

A BIKE WITH TWO WHEELS

I remember to this day the first time I rode a two wheel bike. I would get on and then fall off, on then off again,

and again. My beat-up bike would still shine beauti-
fully, though it had gone through a lot. I kept trying to
ride it until both knees were skinned. Finally I gave
myself one last push and I was riding perfectly through
the breeze.

Ann Boger, *age* 12

Getting started with prose writing is seldom difficult if several
topics are discussed in advance, or if you are working with children who are younger than twelve. Older students are sometimes
inhibited from attempts at writing because they believe they cannot think of anything to write about. They may have been so
often told that writing must have topic sentences and paragraph-
ing that they consider any writing a painful exercise. With
students like these it is important to rediscover that writing can be
fun and to remind them that their own minds are an endless
source of material. A technique to begin a class where students
insist that they can't think of anything to write about is to tell
them that their minds are working all the time, even when they
are asleep. Tell them about the experiments in teaching foreign
language to sleepers by means of earphones. Talk about the different levels of consciousness and remind them that at the same
time we are speaking in sentences to another person we are often
thinking of other things simultaneously at a different level; that
while you are talking about writing you may be worrying about
whether or not you left the keys in the car, that you may also be
hearing the melody from a song played that morning on the
radio. As the students begin to recognize this characteristic of
their own minds, try reading passages from James Joyce to show
how the style of a novel can be constructed using different sorts
of language to demonstrate different levels of wakefulness.

To prove that their own minds are working constantly and that
there is much material in them, ask for cooperation in this experiment: pretend that there is a telephone in front of you, on
the desk or table. Pick it up. What you hear when you put it to

your ear is your own mind working. It will be recording all sorts of stimuli, the sound of traffic outside, colors and textures of clothes, memories, physical discomforts, anxieties. It probably will not be working in sentences. This doesn't matter. Write down everything you hear. You will have to write fast because the mind works fast: it will not slow down for your pencil. It probably will not give you time to spell every word correctly. It does not matter in this assignment because what we want to do is to get a look at what is going on inside your head. Say anything and everything. Write.

There is much excitement generated by this exercise. Assure the class that these exercises will be anonymous. When you finish, ask the students to look over what they have written, and if anyone is willing to pass their papers in, read them aloud. Usually most papers are turned in. Read them at random, careful to point out that this is not an exercise in psychoanalysis but an exercise in looking at the natural style of individual minds. Some people tend to think in verbs, some in verbals, some in rhythms of three-word groups, some in longer rhythms. Some students use their senses extensively to record their surroundings, how things look, smell, and sound nearby. These students will often mention the sound of their own pencil as they write, other noise distractions. Some students will be oblivious to outside stimuli, some will discover an inclination to rhyme, a mind that is playfully nonsensical. All this should be accepted as interesting and fun, an indication of individual differences and a way to better understanding of one's own mind and the natural rhythms of that mind. Further discussion of style in writing is sometimes a natural result of this experiment but it is not necessary since the point of the exercise is to give students who have not had any experience with fluency an opportunity to discover that they have much going on in their heads, more than they can write down, and that planning something to say is not always necessary to creativity.

WHAT'S ON MY MIND

that test
homework
thoroughbreds
horses
our cat
wham, somebody hit the table
blah
water running
mother talking on phone
the television is on
happy story is on
boys
the phone just hung up
my father's mouth is running
silence is golden
gabbing is loud
what now
soft whispers
somebody got up
set a glass or two down
water running
blah

IDEAS FOR WRITING POETRY

All children enjoy poetry. Those few who do not like to write poems are delighted by listening to poems or by "talking poems" of their own. Poetry is the language of feeling, and most of us find deep fulfillment in the expression of our own feelings and listening to the feelings of another person. Working with poetry is a pleasure in the classroom, in small groups, or individually. Some of the reasons might be that poetry is vivid to the mind and the imagination, it sticks in the memory, it demands brief attention, and it involves so much of the poet's and the listener's personality. Poetry is probably more closely related to the way that the mind works than is prose. Succinct, laden with ideas and images, poetry relies upon feeling instead of logic, and permits a freedom of association that is impossible in explanatory talk, or in prose writing.

When beginning to write poetry, it is a handicap to consider form. Attention to form may detract from expression of meaning. Some students may feel that patterns and control are more satisfying than freedom of language. These children will invent their own forms and they can later be instructed in established forms for poetry. But in beginning to discuss or write poems, the most relevant definition is one that emphasizes poetry as an expression of feeling, an attempt to capture one's feelings honestly and to successfully communicate those feelings to another person.

There follow a series of exercises and ideas for the writing of poetry which can also be adapted to use as creative talking or writing of prose.

Activities

Anything that children do because they want to do it can be used as the theme of a poem. Ask them what they do at home or school for fun. Neighborhood play-group activities can be used as topics. For older students, try sports and games such as tobogganing, skiing, swimming, running races, or auto races. Cooking or camping might appeal to some. A campfire or a fire in a fireplace can be suggestive. Write a poem about what can be seen or imagined in the flames. Whatever activities you decide upon, they must have meaning and importance for the students.

DELIVERING PAPERS

Up in the mornin' bout the time of
  six,
I'm out on my bike with my papers
  in my hand.

It's cold outside and I'm ridin'
    slow and I've got to go!
Outside it's like a frozen piece of
    black paper,
All gloomy and dark and cold.
It almost feels like I'm growing old.

      Chip Walpole, *age 10*

CHEERING

My favorite hobby is cheering
And I practice all the time
I want to be a cheerleader
Because they get to go to other schools
And I want to see some other schools.
Cheerleaders dress in orange and blue
Their socks are blue
And make their legs look good.
Cheerleaders have pom poms that they shake
When they say words like:
Spirit, victory, touchdown.
When they holler they say
Go go go
And everybody says it with them
Go go go
Fight fight fight
Shake shake shake
Win win win.

      Debra Culbert, *age 13*

THE SHADOW

See the Shadow, big and black,
if you jump, it jumps back.

      Rand Ellington, *age 7*

Animals

There is potential appeal in some aspect of this subject for almost all ages and groups. Many primary grades study units on animals. The youngest children can respond with love, fear, or interest to a wide range of animals. Try: What would it feel like to be a certain animal? Be a certain animal! The actual presence of the animal in the classroom is effective with the younger student. Concern for ecology extends this interest to high school. Pictures, slides, movies, discussion, or possibly reading some poems about animals inspire older students.

Animals you bring into the classroom have great potential as conversational topics. Matters of safety, hygiene, adequate care of the animal could be discussed. Show your concern for the welfare of the animal. It is fine to let the children stroke and hold the animal if this is practical or possible with the kind of animal you use, but do not let their enthusiasm cause suffering and fear. Watching a goldfish in a bowl can lead to many kinds of poems. What is he doing? Does he like living in the bowl? Does he see you? What does he think of you? The older student might be introduced to this topic by describing the animal and his behavior. Someone will probably introduce his feelings toward the animal or ask a question about the animal's feelings during the discussion. Most ages up to high school would enjoy personifying the animal. What would it say if it could talk? What would you say if you were that animal?

Many primary classrooms are inhabited by one animal or more in connection with science studies. You can use this animal in talking and writing. Students may continue to write about that animal independently.

ANIMALS

The octopus is like a strange
    gray-black table with eight legs.

A rhinoceros is like a monster
    with a knife in his head.
A snake sounds like a water hose
    spurting water in the grass.
A running camel raising sand is
    like a windstorm in the desert.

Allen Thompson, *age 11*

SOFT PUPPY

Soft furry little puppy,
he doesn't have rough paws
like big dogs
just soft paws.
His brown eyes shiver
with chill and fright
his little body is cold,
but inside he is
warm with love.

Patrick Sweeney, *age 11*

THE PIG

Cathy went to Caren's house to
see the crazy pig that had gone
co co. Her name was Caroline.
CRASH! BOOM! slam! BAM!
She had knocked the garbage can
over and all the cans came out:
The Coca-Cola bottle
The bean can
The carrots
And the potato chips.
Caroline decided to eat a potato chip.

CRUNCH! SLURP! She
drank some Coke. Splash, crash, she
dropped it. They gave Caroline
away. She cried and cried and cried
OINK
    OOINK.

Terri M., *age 9*

THE CAT

The cat sips milk,
So daintily,
And walks,
So very quietly.
Her coat is clean,
Her ears are pink,
Her eyes are green,
They do not blink.

Becky Hamel, *age 8*

Most students have or have had a pet. If not, they wish they did. The variety can range from fireflies to horses. A discussion about what kinds of pets people have could open the conversation. Follow the lead of the students. If they start to discuss why some people have certain kinds of pets, take that up. If they seem to want to tell what their pets mean to them, let them do that. It may be that they will want to tell about their pet. If you are taping primary students start soon to ask for verbal poems to record. If you are working with middle elementary, try to encourage as many students as possible to say something. Writing could follow the discussion.

Some small children have imaginary pets they would love to share. What kind of an animal is it? What does it look like? What does it do? What do they feed it? If they do not have an imaginary pet, it will be very easy for them to develop one on the spot because the line between reality and fantasy is not yet tightly drawn. They will vie with one another to create a more and more interesting and satisfactory imaginary pet. Older students will approach this in a more sophisticated manner. They will be more likely to invent a pet they wish they had. You may have to suggest that they make up something that doesn't really exist. In junior high you might ask them to invent the kinds of pets that future generations will have if all the present animals are extinct. They might even want to include the future kinds of people that will have the strange new kinds of pets.

PONY LANGUAGE

I am in the country in the springtime.
The birds are around me.
My pony comes to me.
He speaks his crazy language.
Only I can understand him.
He asks me to repeat every word he says.
And I do.

Kookie Jenkins, *age 12*

MALAMUTE

I went home discouraged
and sat on the couch
when my little puppy
Malamute tumbled on my feet
I reached down
to pet him
he licked my hand
with his warm pink tongue
I looked in his eyes and then
I knew what happiness was.

Dewey Dorsett, *age 10*

MY PET WORM

Once I had a pet worm that
    I found in the rain.
I brought him in the house
    and stuck him in a
    fish bowl that I call
    a worm bowl because
    it has worms in it.
I fed him fish food and
    turtle food and then
    he smelled.
I took him back out
    in the rain and a bird
    ate him.
I bought all that
    food for nothing.

Chris, *age 8*

MY HORSE

There are many kinds of horses, both mean and kind,
But there is no horse like mine.
She jumps; she soars like beauty with wings.
Oh, she is the most wonderful thing.
But this is only a dream and I wish it would come true.
If this would come true, my golden mare would wear
    a saddle of blue.

Beth Seifert, *age 10*

Personified animals can be as much fun as *Alice in Wonderland* or *The Wind in the Willows*. What if we were all animals? What kind of animals would we be? What would we do? What would we say to one another? What if this were a world of animals instead of people? What kind of world would it be? Try the old favorite about the animals going into the Ark. What did they think as they boarded? Choose some particular animal and let him tell about himself and his life. What if some animals you know were people, or could talk like people? What would they say? What would they want us to do for them? What if some of the people you know were animals? With small children this is an easy step for their imaginations. With the middle age group, it may need to be surrounded by a science-fiction aura. If it is going to work in the junior high, it definitely would have to be given some sophistication. For example, create a world in which animals talk and interact like human beings.

A WHITE HORSE

If I were a white horse
I would run in the fields
and children would run after me,
Tell me to stop.
I would let every child ride,
I would be wild,
but nice to children.
When men came to catch me
I would tell the children to hold on
and I would vanish into the white air.

Wild animals fascinate most children. You might share pictures, discuss visits to the zoo, and perhaps tell them things about some wild animal or animals. Their knowledge of the subject may vary from almost none, to a great deal if they are urban children who have visited zoos, or country children who know about the fox, the wolf, and the many small animals that inhabit the edges of our peopled world. Of course, television has supplied an introduction to the idea of wild animals, but this is not as good as direct experience. Descriptions, pretending they are a wild animal, and expressions of emotions toward wild animals are all possible poems at this level. In the middle elementary and junior high, students will also vary in their knowledge of wild animals, depending on experience, reading, and studies in school. A beautiful film, slides, or pictures would help here too. The older ones may be concerned about the welfare of the wild things. Whatever approach they suggest will produce superior talk or writing. There is great appeal in wild animals. Let each one treat the subject individually. If the children have already learned to express themselves fluently, you might try showing some slides, film, or pictures, and then asking them to write about it. You will be amazed at the variety of reaction and expression.

THE ANTELOPE

It is beautiful the way
The antelope moves very swiftly and gracefully
Along the hot plain.
Picture an antelope
Moving in the air,
His legs stretched out behind him
And his front legs stretched out in front.

David Hartley, *age* 11

SPOTS!

If I was a leopard with lots of spots,
I'd look like I had chicken-pox.

Kim Bolick, *age* 7

Ants

If you don't know much about ants, look at an "All About Ants" book or the encyclopedia. It is possible that the children will know more than you do because ants are a subject of considerable fascination for many before speculation and wonder dry up. For a shared experience, you might want to invest in an "ant farm." If you can get out where there is an ant hill, that is useful with small groups. All the children must be able to get close enough to watch the ants at work. It is best if the group is small enough so that they can discuss among themselves what the ants are doing. Taping such comments could result in some interesting poems. By the time they are eleven or twelve years old, children may have begun to lose their interest and respect for ants. However, they can still be moved by knowledge about the organization, industry, and activities of ant colonies.

ANTS

The ants marched
Through the grass
To their home
In the dried grass.
They marched up the
Side and into their home,
Carrying a bug on
Their back
Down, down
They went,
Into their eating
Room.

Richard Abernethy, *age 10*

Any Insect

Well motivated by a slide and a discussion of the habits and life of the insect, good poems can come from elementary and junior high students about any insect. Let the student choose an insect he knows something about (or find out about it beforehand), and discuss it before writing the poems. It might be effective to put the slide on the screen and merely discuss the elements of the picture before writing. For experienced student-poets, try looking at the image and writing poems without prior discussion.

INSECTS

Some people can't remember small
things like insects. Like jungles here,
moss an inch high is like a jungle to a
small insect.

Dewey Dorsett, age 10

PRAYING MANTIS

Praying mantis
Gallant, brave
Rushing off to battle the tall green swords
Held down by the dirt.
He rests on one sword
Looks at the world
His legs stained with blood
From other battles.
Is this the reward
He gets from war?

Denise Chatham, age 13

Birds

Is there a feeder nearby? Can you see it from the windows, or can you go somewhere to sit quietly and watch the birds? There are very fine nature shorts in color available to show if you are city-bound and perhaps lacking in an opportunity to see a live bird. What about those birds? How do they manage with our carelessness, cruelty, and neglect? What would it feel like to be a bird? What about bird families? How do they take care of their babies and each other? In the middle grades, the life of John J. Audubon, his pictures, and conservation concerns could be used to motivate thinking, feeling, talking, and writing on this subject.

GOLDEN WINGS

An eagle flies on golden wings
As golden as the sunset.
It glides with ease,
Yet as fast as a dart.
An eagle seems to spread its wings
Twenty miles apart.
An eagle sets a steady pace,
And eases down on its prey.
An eagle has a mighty claw,
And a beak like a drop of sun.
An eagle weaves a mighty nest,
For an eagle lays a mighty egg
Up upon a cliff.
The eagle has an x-ray eye
With a head of feathers to rest upon.
The eagle flies the speed of a jet,
And the height of the stars.
The eagle's mighty strength
Seems to give it a touch of beauty,
Which no man on this planet
Will ever understand.

Mike Hoke, *age 8*

Fireflies

Very few children fail to be fascinated by the firefly. If fireflies are found where the children live and play, you may be sure that they have thought a great deal about the magic of it. They love Elizabeth Maddox Roberts' poem "Firefly." Sometimes they will confess that they "play" with them by taking their lights off. You will have to decide how you feel about that and what you want to say about it. Children ages nine through twelve might like to write a poem about their experiences with fireflies when they were "little," or make some speculations about why the little bug lights up.

Life in the Oceans

There are some films done from the work of Rachel Carson, the Jacques Cousteau explorations, and others that have to do with food chains and natural balance in the oceans. Encourage the young people to express their emotions about what they see. Some will be horrified that so much of nature is "eat and be eaten." Some will respect the rational order of it all. Since this subject will of necessity deal with indirect experience, it is too difficult for the younger child. It is suitable for upper elementary. Its usefulness in high school depends a great deal on its presentation. This kind of material is sophisticated, but if it can be related by the parent, poet, or teacher to understanding and emotional response, it can result in constructive conversation, and good writing. Try this if you know quite a bit about it, love it, and want to share it.

THE BIGGEST FISH I CAUGHT

Once I caught a little Trout,
A Bass caught it
A Musky got the Bass
A Barracuda got the Musky
A Tarpon got the Barracuda
A Tuna got the Tarpon
A Sailfish got the Tuna

A Shark got the Sailfish
A Whale got the Shark
And all this happened in a pail
In my backyard.

Bill Wright, *age 10*

TV Animals

Representations of real animals like Lassie, and cartoon animals should be avoided. All you will get is repeats of things children have seen and heard. If students suggest using TV animals, it might be a good time to discuss whether or not TV lets you use your imagination or whether it does all the work for you so that you can't see it your own way.

Toads, frogs, turtles, snakes, chameleons, and other lizards and amphibians

Creatures such as these could be presented in various ways. A close-up view of a horned toad may not be unlike a view of a terrible monster to a small child. The way children respond to the experience of seeing one of these animals depends on their age and past experience, as well as their scientific interest. It would be fun to listen to a group talk about how the toad looks to them and how they feel about it. Some students may have played with such animals enough to have an easy relationship and even affection for them. They may have a great deal of information about the animal's life. Other students may be frightened or repelled by the same animal. Write or talk a poem describing the creature, the students' experiences with it, or his feelings about it. Perhaps some other aspect will be suggested to you as the students talk. Some students might enjoy writing about an experience they once had with one of these creatures. If the talk turns to monsters, you might start talking and writing poems about monsters.

LIZARDS

Lizards are funny things
They sit upon the ground.
When they crawl around,
They never make a sound.

Timmy B., *age 11*

Apologies

Because all of us have regrets, writing a poem of apology captures the imagination of older students who find it difficult to
express their feelings of being sorry. Younger children are also
pleased with this subject if they are made aware that they can
admit or say anything without censorship, or that they might in
fact apologize for deeds they have thought of committing.

I have put your fish
down the drain
Forgive me,
They were so ugly,
so slippery and wet
They kind of went down
by themselves.

Sherry McGinnis, *age 10*

I am sorry I pushed
you down in the mud
I'm sorry if you got hurt
and for being so mean
I am going
to let you come

over to my house
all the week long.

Jackie Hinton, *age 10*

Biographies and Fictitious Diaries

There are many ways to approach this exercise as talk, poetry, or prose. It is a favorite because children get to use the subject they know most about, themselves. Elementary school children enjoy making up stories about their lives which include the future, predictions of marriage, career, glamor and death. Older students like to imagine they are someone else, perhaps enlivening studies in history and science by writing the diary of that person on the day of a special event: Lincoln on the day of the Gettysburg Address, Amelia Earhart on the day of her first flight, Columbus halfway to the New World.

TONOIMATACHUMAPHALA

If I were an Indian I would love it.
I would go fishing every day
even though I know I'm a girl.
My flag would be blue with a
green-spotted brook trout on it.
I have a favorite time,
it is when I ride my palomino pony.
The pony is white with black and brown
spots.
I have a pet monkey
his name is Matachono.
My name is Tonoimatachumaphala
But they call me Wild Green Fields
That Blow In The Breezes.
I like my life.

Joy Smith, *age 10*

EPITAPH OF JONATHAN FOSTER

Jonathan Foster died today
He was 83
He worked for 40 years
Sometimes he made clothes
He lived in a good house
He drove a GTO
He was handsome
He died in a car wreck
His wife was with him
She didn't get hurt
And neither did the GTO.

Jonathan Foster, *age 10*

Communication

Communication with another person, the opportunity and experience of expressing one's feelings and thoughts, is a subject of deep concern to children and young people. There are several exercises which facilitate this. One of the best is to suggest that the student or child write a poem to someone to whom he wants to express something and has not been able to do so. This could be a friend, someone in his family, some famous person, either living or dead, to whom he feels some indebtedness, some opposition, something he would like to argue. A young scientist might write a letter or a poem to Einstein, to Marie Curie, or the local director of last year's science fair. A young artist might write a letter to the artist to whom he would most like to express his admiration, Michelangelo perhaps, or Flip Wilson. An interesting response to this assignment was a poem written by a sixteen-year-old to people in the world whom she knew she would never get to meet. She named them in the manner of Walt Whitman and told them that she wished she could know them all.

COMMUNICATION AT SCHOOL

The teachers stand
And students sit
And never come together.

Deenie Fleishman, *age 14*

PHILOSOPHY

Talk
With someone.
It lets out all emotions.
Joy is seldom prominent
Self-pity is usually dominant.

Dorothy Hull, *age 17*

I want to write this poem
And make it say what I mean
Come on words, feelings . . . why
Stay in my narrow confining head
When the sunshine, the flowers
And kind faces want to know
What is in my heart?

Lou McAlister, *age 18*

He needed
somebody to
lean on,
confess to,
to share the
happiness
and disappointments

of growing up,
to open up
and share
his inner feelings
with. An
honest
but strange
hope came that there would be
a new-found
friend who
would not be only
hearing,
but understanding.
He needed
someone to
love him;
a girl;
or even a boy—somebody;
someone;
a friend;
a buddy;
but—
no one
would listen.

Julie Hicks, *age 13*

MOMENT

I stand on your steps;
I hear you crying quietly inside . . .
And I want to tell you
About a flower I touched on my walk over,
And take you outside and show you
The color of a bird perched on your picket fence,
And let you hear him whistle in the wind

Before he flies away . . .
I've no time to stand and wonder
What spring looks like
From the other side of the sky.
But still I'm afraid to knock . . .
Not knowing whether my happiness
Would come to you like
Hot cocoa when you've been in the snow,
Or blinding light when you've been sleeping.

Anonymous student, *age 16*

Comparisons

Some of the most imaginative conversations and writing can come from making comparisons of one thing to another. This exercise is often stimulated by a shared experience. The classroom teacher might use something like an eggbeater or give each child a blade of grass and follow up with questions like: What does this sound like or feel like; how does it taste? It is also effective to read poems to the class, pointing out that much of poetry depends on making vivid comparisons of one thing to another. Parents who are aware of language enrichment can use this exercise often. To point out that the broccoli does look like little trees, that rocks are like mountains, and hands are like tools establishes a way of perception that enriches thought. The exercise of making comparisons lends itself to limited or extensive treatment in conversation, prose, or poetry.

COMPARISONS

My sister is like a match (She has red hair and is skinny).
A spider is like a blot of black ink spilled on the floor.
When I am mad, I am like a teakettle
    ready to burst.

When my eyes are closed, it looks like
    a foggy night in New England.

       Shirley Burgess, *age 12*

When I look at the trees
    they look like scarecrows
      waving their arms through the breeze.
When I look at snakes
    they look like beautiful blue waves
      rolling in the ocean.
A hippopotamus looks like a big river
    with gray water.
And a big brown bear looks like a big
    tree trunk when it is standing still.

       Diana Greene, *age 9*

The letter C reminds me
    of half of an egg.
A light bulb reminds me
    of the sun showing through
    the glass.
The letter Q reminds me of a man
    with a cigar
    hanging out of his mouth.
The stars in the sky
    remind me of the
    Dallas Cowboys.
The word crazy is like
    my dog.

       Jim Weston, *age 11*

The thread was stacked like bricks in a wall.
A feather floats like the clouds in the sky.

THE SCHOOL AGE CHILD

The boys were excited
    like bears that found
    honey.
The letter i is like a
    cannon going off.

        Brad Cox, *age 11*

A chain saw sounds like a woodpecker
    that can't stop.
Someone coughing sounds like the wind
    banging the shutters.

        William Morris, *age 10*

THE RIVER

Life is a river
of happenings
and experiences
forever washing and being fed
and flowing
to the sea

        Rob White, *age 16*

Color

    Children have fun observing colors and using them in different kinds of poems. Be careful with the youngest ones because some of them won't know their colors yet. Any poem which uses sense experiences can include ideas of color. Color can also be used as the main ingredient of a poem. What is color? Blue is like . . . Make similes with any color. Relate color experiences with other sense experiences or with emotions. How does red taste? How does pink feel to the touch? How does green smell? How does purple move? How does orange sound? How do specific colors make you feel emotionally? Also, you can write a yellow poem. You might have fun using a bouquet of colors in a poem, and dealing with each color in relation to a specific sense or emotion. If you use this topic with older students you might need to preface it by discussing word-associations or idea-associations. High school students might accept an introduction that included some psychological concepts concerning color. You will probably have best results with color in the lower grades where imaginations are more free.

BLACK
(A talked poem)

Black is proud.
Black is pretty.
Black is soul.
Black is my color.
When somebody kisses me I feel black
all over.

Larry Gillespie, *age* 7

A POEM ABOUT COLORS

Blue makes me feel like I am a big cloud floating in the sky
Blue makes me feel like a sponge
Yellow makes me feel like a sunny day
It makes me feel happy
Like eating a banana
Like combing my hair.
Red makes me feel hot and furry
Red makes me think there are dots in front of my eyes.
Gray makes me bored and tired
Pink makes me feel young
Green makes me feel clean

Black makes me feel scared
White feels like socks
Silver makes me feel like a piece of chalk scratching
    on the blackboard
On different days I feel different ways
When I'm dark I feel fierce
When I'm light I feel cheerful.

Collaboration poem, *8 and 9 year old children*

COLORS

Colors, colors, all around
Blue, green, yellow, brown
Red, purple, gold, or white
They all go away
When you turn off the light.

Richard Mack, *age 8*

PURPLE

Purple purple I'm purple
Purple head Purple heart
Purple teacher Purple poet
Purple purple purple
Julian purple Jerita purple
Julian Jerita oh oh
I think I'm going to faint.

Florita Harris, *age 10*

GRAY

Gray is an elephant.
Gray is a time
I've spent in my tent.

Gray is the smoke
    that comes out of your
    mouth on a cold day.
Gray is the clouds
    on the way
    to my fort.
Gray is a shadow
    on the street.
Gray is a
    kind-of-dirty
       feet.

        Jamie Chapin, *age 8*

blue
the patterns of my mind intermingle
    with the colored words
       of your blue day
reaching out to the aura of your world
old patterns fade away
    heavier shades of navy
       the opaqueness of the winter sky
lie shattered in mirrored fragments of blue.

        Leslie Boney, *age 17*

RED

Red is a cushion
On the bed
Red is the stop light
That says, "Don't go ahead."
Red is a soda
In your mouth
Red is the sunset
In the South.

Red is a feeling
People like.
Red is the color
Bulls fight.
Red is tomato juice
In a can.
Red is a juicy
Piece of ham.

Charles McCullough, *age 8*

THE COLORS OF LOVE

Red is a color of sorrow,
    hurt, pain.
Love is red, white, and blue,
    all flashy with stars,
with sudden streaks of yellow.

Crystal Lunsford, *age 12*

Current Events

Newspapers, radio, and television are full of things that catch
the students' attention. Educational television has regular news
programs that might be available for some classes. Much of this
can be used with discretion and imagination as ideas for poems.
Floods, fires, and contests make good topics. You can use elec-
tions or trials. War is a deep concern with many groups. Be sure
you have some conception of what is the latest sensation in current events locally, because often the most violent and unnatural
news grips the students. You may not want to handle it, or you
may not feel equipped to handle these topics in a constructive
way.

YESTERDAY IN THE PAPER

There was a picture of a dog
Who had lost her puppies in a fire.
Her master whom she loved
Started out doing one thing
But ended up doing another.
He meant to keep them warm with a light
But he was careless.
Now she lies there, not eating,
Not drinking, in the ashes of her children.

Matt Troxler, *age 12*

Description

Inasmuch as imagery is one of the elements of poetry, descriptions lend themselves well as themes for poems. A description of anything that you think has possibilities could be used. Don't choose something unless you are excited about its potential for interesting description. You might bring things into the classroom. Pictures: reproductions of masters, originals, including children's originals, pictures from magazines, or pictures from the school library and local public library; any art object: figurines, decorated bowls, beautiful vases, or fabric; any utensil or tool of everyday life familiar to the group—toothbrush, hair brush, egg beater, hammer, farm tool. Try something from nature: a flower, a stick, leaf, or a blade of grass. There might be something already in the classroom you can use, but be sure that it is interesting and you think you can help the children to see it with new eyes.

You might take a short walk outside of the school building. What do you see that you can describe? Is there an interesting building (perhaps even the school), an interesting planting, tree, or a weathered fence you can use? If you are in a factory or urban district, what is there to describe that has interesting color, shape, sound, texture, or smell? Don't restrict yourself to adjective ideas. Consider what happened before your observation and what will happen after your observation at any point in time. Drawing a "word picture" of something nearby makes a good talk too. Close attention to the object required is an exercise in increasing awareness. Descriptions can be varied from the simplest treatment for kindergarten, "It is like . . ." to very sophisticated, philosophical ideas for the oldest students. An example is Robert Frost's comparison of life to a road.

When a window is open
it is like a giant mouth
eating up the air.

Andy Whitson, *age 10*

Lightning looks like white color
crayon
Drawing a crooked line down a
dark night.

Ned Yount, *age 10*

A path is a narrow tunnel with
no roof that gets you where you're
going faster but harder.
A fence is a fort around a King's
castle, but when you stop playing
It's just a plain old fence.

Tony Leary, *age 10*

BRIDGE

A bridge is like a big boat taking you across waters
It is like a rainbow without pretty colors
It is like a half apple or orange
That you cannot eat.

Wilma Capehart, *age 10*

MARTIN'S HEAD

Martin's head looks like a playground.
His nose is like a long slide.
His hair is the swings.
His mouth is the tunnel to nowhere.
His eyes are the merry-go-round
forever rolling.
His eyelashes are monkey bars.
His cheeks are beds of red roses.
His neck is a long, thin climbing pole.
His ears are mazes.

Debbie Jordan, *age 10*

Dreams—Sleep—Lullabies

Dreams make a good topic for all grade levels. The fun of dream poems is that they are so different one from another. They can be full of sense experiences and fantasy at the same time. One way to introduce this idea is to ask the students to tell something about their dreams. Don't let them start telling the whole story of a dream because it will take up too much time. Be specific in what you ask. Do you remember a special dream that you enjoyed? What did you like about it? Do you remember a special dream that frightened you? What was so frightening about it? Have you ever had a nightmare? Have you ever dreamed something and then awakened to believe it had really happened?

Have you ever awakened from a dream and thought you were still dreaming? Have you had a dream that you wish were true? Have you ever had the same dream over and over? If you can't remember a special dream you want to write about, can you make up a dream?

There might be some problem in talking and writing about dreams for older students. They might feel that the topic is too personal or embarrassing or they might want to analyze their dreams and begin to get into topics which are not constructive and perhaps disturbing. This can be avoided by suggesting that they talk or write about dreams that they had a long time ago.

Last night I had a dream,
It was about a horse that I had got.
The color of it was black,
It felt very soft,
And it didn't make a sound.

Sharon Walker, *age 10*

THE VALLEY OF BLUE

As I was walking through the blue valley
I came upon a grape vine
It went all through the valley
I peered through the thick vine with my beady eyes
And I saw a huge, black and green creature
With white shining claws and spikes down its warty back.
All of a sudden
People appeared
With hair down to their ugly toes.
When one brave man tried to take the creature alone
The creature left him lying on the ground in a puddle of
    blood.

Others had the same grief
And alas only a few got away
And so did I
The valley of blue is a place of blood
But it's only a dream.

Jerry Patterson, *age 13*

Sleep topics are closely related. Have you ever walked in your sleep? Have you ever seen anyone walk in his sleep? Make up a sleepwalking incident. Have you ever had trouble falling asleep? While you lie awake, what did you think about, and what did you see and hear in the dark? What about waking-up times? Have you had any special experiences waking up? Have you ever awakened and not known where you were?

SLEEP

When you are falling off to sleep and
    you barely hear a basketball
game on television,
    it sounds like bees buzzing.
Sometimes when my mother closes a drawer
    in the kitchen it sounds like
my sister lifting the lid off the cookie jar
    to get the last cookie that was
supposed to be mine.

Jan Allen, *age 11*

Tender lullabies can be written by some students. If there is a small baby in the home, this can be an experience poem. In elementary grades, what about a lullaby for a pet, after discussing how and where the animal goes to sleep. What does the pet dream?

LULLABIES

I have a cat with soft, soft fur
When night time comes to make her purr
This is the song I sing to her:
"Sleep little cat, don't make a sound
Dream of Springtime all around
And your soft paws on the warm green ground."

Tony Aspland, *age 9*

Dear little eagle shut your eyes
Tomorrow is going to be grand
Your feathers are grown and you can fly
with nothing to stop you.

Bruce Rinehart, *age 9*

One night I went to feed my gerbels
And they were scared
So I said
"Little Gabe, little Heather,
Don't be afraid
I came to feed you
So you won't be hungry
So you won't be scared."

Jamie Chapin, *age 9*

Ecology

A natural sense of wonder about nature makes children especially sensitive and concerned for the things in nature. They seem to have a special insight into the importance of ecological balance and love to discuss or write about this topic.

A SILENT SPOT

I wandered into a silent spot
That seems to last forever,
I hear the birds
Singing their own words.

One bird was hard to see
Perhaps he's just a dream
A dream very thoughtful
Full of bliss and solitude.

I looked until I saw
A lonely dead stump
Calling to me with a
Mourning voice.

I heard the wind rustling
Through the leaves,
With a whisper saying,
"Go on, Go on."

I went on farther,
But to my sadness
I saw litter which men
Threw out, with madness.

Chip Sisk, *age 10*

IN THE WOODS

Have you ever, my friend
seen a tree, a little tree, a little
tree. Have you ever seen a tree
just a tree just for me.
Have you ever touched
a leaf, a little leaf, a tiny leaf?

Have you ever touched
a leaf, a green leaf, a green leaf?
Have you ever touched a satin leaf, a satin
leaf?
Have you ever seen all my
wonders, all my wonders, all my wonders,
all my wonders, if you haven't, my
friend, seen all my wonders, all my wonders.
They may not be here tomorrow.

Michael Leighton, *age 11*

I am the grass,
the trees,
the dirt,
the air,
I am the world.
If you, yes, you
Do not take care of me
If you do not clean up this mess
You, man
Will die.

Cindy Jones, *age 10*

The Indians' song of sorrow is in the woods
Trying to sing back Nature's goods.

Bill Whedon, *age 11*

Emotions

Encouragement to express emotions can result in good poems.
All the kinds of love experienced by the various age groups can
be considered. Love will be a popular topic with high school

students because of their preoccupation with boy-girl relations. Read aloud good examples of love poems before they write. Special care should be taken to accept all their attempts without criticism, and allow opportunity for anonymity if reading and sharing these poems.

"Happiness is . . ." poems are easy, and most groups can have fun with them. Don't be afraid to use this with students in any circumstances. Suggest that they write about the things that make them happy. Smiles and laughter make a good topic too.

"How do you feel about . . . ?" can start older children into poems about their own feelings regarding anything that is emotionally charged for them. Unhappy or "bad" feelings can be topics of a poem. Students have experiences of fear or cruelty that can be expressed and better understood in a poem. For the younger students, ask: Has anyone ever been mean to you? How did it make you feel? What mean things do you sometimes feel like doing? Write a poem about the time your feelings were hurt.

HAPPINESS

Happiness is a sailboat gliding
    across the sea.
Happiness is the X-15 at your
    controls.
Happiness is building the thing
    you've always wanted.
Happiness is admiring your
    creation.
Happiness is solitude.

Sam Deal, *age 13*

A POEM

Today is gloomy.
I like it and dislike it.

I don't know why.
Trees so still,
dark, deep sky.
But it lets you notice
How animals feel.
They're timid, afraid,
But they still move.
They walk along a phone wire
Made of steel.

Kit Linden, *age 10*

Fear is a thundercloud crackling,
Fear is a lightning bolt's flash,
Fear is a hair-raising story
     where men turn to
     creatures that are burnt
     into ash.

Dick Ridenhour, *age 13*

I am the wind blowing free
through the big meadow full of the
smell and the beauty of daisies.
I hear my mother calling, I must
lock this feeling in a little box.

Kevin Riley, *age 13*

HAPPINESS IS

Happiness is getting a pet
Happiness is going to the movies
Happiness is not going to the dentist
Happiness is like getting your allowance

Happiness is eating a watermelon
Happiness is having a good time.
But most of all happiness is
    getting new shoes that fit.

Donald Waters, *age 10*

There were spiders
all over
my back, my face
They chased me out of the room
I ran until
he came
There, he said,
cry,
tell me
I wanted to but . . .
Not even he . . .
He said well sleep then

And the spiders came back

Julia Poirier, *age 13*

HAPPINESS

Happiness is being a sled
and moving to Alaska.
Or being a dull pencil, and
being in love with the pencil sharpener.

Happiness is a hot day,
and a cold coke.
It's a lonely beachball
on the way to the beach.

Happiness is thinking it's Friday
and remembering it's Saturday.

It's wanting your sister to have twins
and getting triplets.

Jules Buxbaum, *age 13*

I'M GLAD TO GET AWAY FROM YOU

Before I leave for
Hawaii I'd just like
to say that . . .
I'll be glad to get away from you for
once in my life, because you are a
terrible person to be with. You are the
only person I want to get away from, so
don't expect a letter or anything from me.
Good-by!

Melony Price, *age 9*

FEELING BORED

I have a feeling,
it's a dark feeling.
I don't want to play the
games in the closet.
I don't want to go outside
it's too hot. When I pick up my
book I can't read it thinking my
friend is on a beautiful palomino
in the beautiful graceful wind
while I'm sick in bed.

Lea Cahoon, *age 10*

SIMPLE!

It takes so little to make a person happy
or a dog
or a cat

or a lizard
or a spider
or a frog
or a fish . .

. .

. .

. .

Anonymous student, *age 14*

Free
Is being able
To
Jump
Without falling.

Ginger Allen, *age 12*

Future—Past

Real understanding of past, present, and future is slow to develop. The older students will do better with these topics, though you might find some ways to simplify and adapt them for the younger students. Starting with the past, you might suggest poems relating to the period of history being studied by the class. Particular people or particular events might be good. Putting yourself into the past is fun and can result in good poems if the class understands the period about which it is writing. What would you have been doing one hundred years ago in this town or that town? Many ages would enjoy "being" a cave man and writing a poem about their life. If you want to use the past of the student's life, you might try titles like: "The first thing I remember in my life," "A memorable event in my life," or "My most embarrassing moment."

The individual future of pupils and the collective future of humankind is a genuine concern of older elementary through high school youth. What kind of a future do you want to have? Where will you be one year from now, or ten years from now? What will you be doing? What would you like to be when you grow up? From about age twelve on, students think about marriage. They might describe their future husband or wife or write a poem about a marriage.

WHEN I LEARNED TO COUNT

Several years ago
When I was six or seven
I learned to count
to nearly a thousand.

I felt like the smartest boy ever
Since 1000 was such a BIG number,
So I tried it one night
Got to 500, then started to slumber.

Mike Myers, *age 12*

SOMEDAY

In the future
I will never get married.
People think
If you can cook eggs
You will get married.
I have cooked eggs since I was seven
And I get bored
With people who say
I will change my mind someday
And get married.

Julia Willis, *age 10*

FUTURE LIFE

I looked out with my mind
And what did I see?
I saw my life stretched
Out before me.

I thought to myself
As I looked out,
"What in the world
Will my life be about?"

I want to watch
The moon on the lake.
I want to hear birds
Each day when I wake.

I want to run,
Free with the land.
All by myself
On the burning sand.

I want to sit
Near a bubbling creek,
Where I wonder
What do I seek?

I want a life
Uncluttered with crime,
Pollution, death, people,
Common things in my time.

But now I know
Very well, indeed,
That this won't be
The life I'll lead.

Mary Davidson, *age 14*

Gender

Young students are especially conscious of the privileges and inequities imposed upon them because of gender. Attitudes toward being male or female are interesting to analyze and poems which examine this topic can be fun as well as constructive of tolerance.

WHY I HATE TO BE A GIRL

I hate to be a girl.
A girl is fancy lace and perfume
But if you ask me, it stinks.

A girl gets to do house work with her mamma
But I would rather play softball.

Kim Huff, *age 13*

IT'S BEST TO BE A BOY

Girls get to be first
But not much else.
Girls only think about clothes
And want to look fantastic all the time.
I don't feel anything about clothes
Except I like to wear my clothes
All hanging off
And my name on my jacket.
Boys feel important
I don't ever want to take a girl out
I want somebody to take me out.

Jimmy Thomas, *age 11*

GIRLS

A girl's mouth
A forever-playing phonograph.

A girl's mind
An undecided barrel full
of unbelievable wishes.

Mike Durham, *age 14*

Happenings—events

Events that stand out in our individual memories or our collective memory can be used as topics for poems. Consider the significant happenings in the lives of the group with which you are working: the death of a public figure; ceremonies and religious experiences; carnivals, circuses, and county fairs. The subject could be something special that affected the individual somehow. Maybe it was an accident, suffered or witnessed. Maybe it was a party. It could even be something that happened at recess!

WORDS FROM 1773

We want freedom!
Was the demand.
We don't want to be
    Englishmen.
We won't pay a sum
    of money on tea,
We'd rather drown in the sea.

Russ Robinson, *age 10*

THE PHOTOGRAPHER

A camera man came to our room
Took a picture of us with a zoom

The picture he got
Surprised him a lot
It was me and my friend
Making faces at him.

Anonymous, *age 10*

MY PET

I had a skunk
So soft and small,
A white stripe down her back.
She ran after me each day
And with me she went on walks,
We had fun!
One night I went out
To feed my little pet,
She was dead,
I was sad,
Tears came to my eyes,
My wonderful pet was dead!

Ann Thomas, *age 10*

Holidays—Seasons

Holidays are not to be ignored, especially since they are such an easy topic. What does Christmas mean to you? . . . or Easter? . . . or Hanukkah? . . . or whatever holiday coming next on the calendar is generally observed by the group with which you are working. Maybe it will be Flag Day or Thanksgiving. Discuss the meaning of the holiday with the students. Don't let the discussion last too long. When a student begins to want to tell a story about a particular celebration or a particular person, it is a sign that the discussion should end. Some poets have suggested that it is less interesting to write a poem after it has been explicitly spoken.

Many good poems have already been written about particular holidays. You might read several related poems the day before the students write. If you read to them just before they write, it will diminish the originality of their work. If you read the poems the day before they write, then your discussion can include a discussion of those poems. Don't rely solely on the students' knowledge of the holiday and start out by saying, "Let's write a poem about Halloween," for example. You will be disappointed with the results.

THANKS ON THANKSGIVING

I am thankful to have places that are fun
Like SIX FLAGS
Or DISNEY LAND

I am thankful for brave people
Like Buffalo Bill
Wild Bill Hickok
And Astronauts.

I am thankful for inventors
Like Benjamin Franklin
George Washington Carver

I am thankful for people who make me happy
Like Flip Wilson
The Osmond Brothers
The Jackson 5.

I am thankful for people who like me
Like David Hartley
Steve Leighton
Mark Miller
And Jeff Gorelick.

Mike Flood, *age 10*

THANKSGIVING

God, I thank you for my dogs.
If You hadn't made them
I wouldn't have anyone to greet me after school.

Cindy Jones, *age 10*

HALLOWE'EN

The Night was cold;
    and very dark.
The spooks were prowling
    through the park.

A big black cat up in a tree;
Scared the living daylights
    out of me.

Gus Clark, *age 10*

CHRISTMAS

Christmas is a time of embarrassment
When you get someone Skittle Pool
And they get you a used Peanuts book.
Christmas is vacation for children,
Shopping for Mother and a money shortage for Dad.
Christmas has too much Santa and too little God.

Greg Baer, *age 10*

THE EASTER LILY

Silent and mysterious stood the Easter flower
In her long, light robes of green, waiting.
"Who are you?" asked the bees as they flew on by.

"Who are you?" asked the roses from their bed.
"Please tell us!" begged the butterfly.
"I am a light that shines for Easter Day."

Nori Roden, *age 10*

Poems could be written about one of the four seasons with its sights, sounds, smells, and activities. The months make good topics for poems. What happens during a certain month? Try using the times of day: dawn, high noon, afternoon, twilight, or night.

FALL

The crickets, the birds,
The spiders, the bugs,
Are all getting ready
For something or other.

Emmie Keesler, *age 10*

SPRING

In the small but frequent showers,
Birds sing in the mist
from huge trees.

David Miller, *age 10*

I AM TWILIGHT

I am twilight
I see the first awakening stars peeping from their
      misty beds of enshrouded daytime.
I feel the cool mists of night gently sweeping over the
      heated clouds of day.

And now I see the moon coming alive, shining and
    shimmering with the light of the reflected sun, and
I know I must die only to be reborn tomorrow once
    more.

        Catherine Mesrobian, *age 17*

WHEN SPRING COMES

When spring comes
I find a sunny spot,
where the grass is tall,
with a little stone for my head,
Where the trees meet the sky,
Casting a shadow over the ground.
Spring is here,
And the weather is fair.
So the rabbits come out of their lair.
Bees buzz,
and bears lose their fuzz,
And flowers get back their buds.

        Worth Burke, *age 10*

Spring is dancing and prancing on the grass,
Sit down by the spring
And put your tired feet in it and rest,
And a butterfly comes and sits down in your lap.

        Angelia Greeson, *age 11*

Humor

Children are naturally playful with language and all students
love jokes. Young writers should be encouraged to play with
language and ideas but an exercise in being funny is difficult.

Those who are adept at humor are stimulated to produce funny poems when given an opportunity to experiment with the personification of animals or inanimate objects, or by listening to the humorous poems and ideas of other children or of good poets.

PINE CONE

If a pine cone was alive
He would say pricky things
If you touched him you'd say ouch.
He is always lonely because if
you try to talk to him he says
pricky things like shutup, you
fool and you don't know what you're
saying.

Leila Maglione, *age 10*

SQUARE HEADS

Some people's heads are square
as picture frames,
Since most of them are wood,
They would float on water good.

Steve Maglione, *age 10*

If I were a clock
Instead of ringing
I would holler
for everyone to get up.

Wendy Cooper, *age 10*

Don't hit my yellow and blue meow.
Put orange swimmers in the tank.

Shoot that red horn
And pat my bark—
He won't bite.

Selina Pate, *age 10*

I have worn
your clothes
and torn them

I wore them
to a Halloween party
to see who could be the tackiest

And guess what?!
I won!

Enite Nance, *age 10*

FREDDIE, THE FRIENDLY FAT
FUNNY-FACED FROG

I'm Freddie the friendly fat
funny-faced frog.
They call me Freddie for short.
I have soft green skin
Filmy as eyeballs.
When I breathe
it sounds like a burp.

David Rea, *age 11*

IF RATS COULD TALK

If rats could talk
they would say,
This is a stick up!

Empty your refrigerator!
They would take cheese and run away
and that's what would happen if rats could talk.

Marilyn Turnage, *age 10*

Identity—Self-Image

This is a captivating topic to use with older children. The older
the student, the closer he is to a real need to explore his identity.
He may not want to share his poems, not even with the teacher-
poet, but he will welcome the invitation to write about such questions as: Who am I? What am I? What am I worth? What is
going to happen to me? What should I do with my life? Is there
any hope for me to accomplish something important in life? Am
I really no good, as everyone seems to think sometimes? What's
the use of living?

You do not need to suggest the questions. Those that need
answers are already in the unspoken language of the child's mind.
Motivation can be provided by suggesting that the students write
about themselves and the things they think about or worry about.
If you have permission to read some of their poems back to the
group, and you do so sympathetically and reassuringly, it will
further unloose an outpouring of identity poems. This is the kind
of poem children will go on writing and which is especially helpful to adults trying to understand a child or to the adolescent
trying to understand himself.

For the younger ones, it might be helpful to suggest that they
use similes and metaphors to express their ideas about themselves.
Suggest that they compare what they seem to be to a metaphor
for what they really are. Try having them compare themselves
to someone or something. If you could choose to be anyone or
anything you wanted to be, who or what would you choose?
"Growing up" begins to be a concern at a very young age. If
one of the students uses that term in the discussion before writing, don't be afraid to use it too.

My daddy thinks of me
as a monkey.
My mother thinks I'm a pest.
There's a cave in my body
That no one can touch.
It's my secret.

Marilyn Turnage, *age 10*

I think of the moon as a spoon of potatoes.
I think of the sun as a yellow pea.
Some people think of me
as a sad little boy,
but I am really a happy one.

Bobby Kenney, *age 10*

I used to be a bluebird.
Now I am a bird with a broken wing.

Michele Alexander, *age 10*

I seem to be noisy as a train
but I am really quiet as the grass.

Kenneth Rankins, *age 10*

I seem to be a picture
but I am really a book
a mouth full of words
a bowl full of shoes.

Blake Boyce, *age 10*

I used to be surrounded by the Pacific Ocean but
now I'm wound up in a spider's web.

> Jane Terry, *age 9*

I used to crawl on my knees,
But now I climb trees.

> Bruce Rinehart, *age 8*

I used to be a sky
    all blue and clean
But now I'm a curtain
    hanging black with grief.

> Tena Lay, *age 14*

I used to be
a girl of different
ways of living.
Different ways of getting along.
When I was
small
my person-
ality was like
the waves of
the ocean that
creeps up against
the sandy shore.
My feelings almost
as though they
were made of
sugar
when they were hurt

very easily I could almost
feel it melt
and run
down my
cheek. But
now I'm
like a tree
that's sprouted
into a beautiful
dogwood.

Lois Little, *age 14*

ME

I was born in Virginia or maybe,
        Tennessee
I guess I'm nothing to you,
But to me I'm me.
I work all day,
I sleep all night
Maybe I will play someday,
Well I might!
I love my blue jeans
When my mother throws out a pair,
It's always a fight.
My name is Leslie,
And your name is monkey.
I wish I had a pizza,
I wish I were Cinderella,
and got whatever I want.

Leslie Fry, *age 11*

ABOUT MYSELF

When I was a little boy I always ate mud,
When I was three I bit my mother's leg,

When I was 7 I hated spinach,
When I was nine I loved shrimp
My favorite clothes are bell bottoms
I was born in South Carolina,
I am now ten and living in North Carolina,
When I am 25 I am going to be a policeman,
When I die, I will die at a movie.

Billy Shaw, *age 10*

MY SELF

Once upon a time there was a girl
        name Chris Harris
That is me
My sister call me dogeyes
My mother did too
I thought I was not dogeyes
I beats up my sister when she call
        me that
I beats her to death.

Chris Harris, *age 11*

Inventions

An invention is something that is thought up, thought out, produced, or originated. It is a good word to use with the older students, but primary children will love the word "pretend," or "make-believe." Middle elementary children might prefer the word "invent," and from there on up, you would certainly need to say invent. There is no limit to this topic. Blow a soap bubble and ask the children to invent a world inside the bubble. Invent a new world anywhere! Invent a different kind of life for humankind or for yourself. Invent a new race of people, or invent a new you! Invent a new language, a strange day in your life, or a miracle. See how unusual, practical, beautiful, or frightening

a thing you can invent. Invent something you wish you had or
wish you could do.

I AM AN INVENTOR

I'm going to invent
A portable house with a portable roof.
It will have compact chairs
And accordion stairs.
Push-in spigots
And a folding sink,
Pretty clever, don't you think?
Each room turns into a tiny cube
Smaller than an innertube.
Each cube fits a tiny case
Smaller than a lion's face.
No matter how large or small your home
When completed it looks like chrome.

Elizabeth McMillan, *age 12*

MY SUPER PLANE

My plane is all the different colors in the world.
It is made of feather wings
and fish scales for the body.
It is shaped like a whale with wings,
but my plane doesn't fly.
That is what is so bad about my plane.
I have to paddle anywhere I go.

Jacqueline Hines, *age 10*

THE WEATHER MACHINE

I'm going to invent a weather machine
I'll press a button to make it go.
And for one whole year it will snow.

Anonymous

Music

Almost everyone responds to music. Many young people talk about rock music and their favorite groups, so it is often easy to discuss or write about music. It can be exciting to write down anything that comes into your head while listening to music. Different kinds of music produce different images and emotions. A comparison of Bach's music to the music of a contemporary favorite like Bob Dylan can increase awareness and vocabulary.

If you use music on records, you can explain that a composer tries to create images, tell a story, or express emotions with his art form. As the students listen, they can write a poem that says in words what they think the composer is saying, or they can write what the music says to them. Lyrics interfere with success in writing poems to music. Motivating poems with music is difficult, but can be done in any grade level if the students are given the necessary background and the teacher has the skill. Music teachers might be able to help with suggestions and records.

MUSIC

Music is like a
flower singing in
the wind. Music
is like a bird
singing to his
wife. It is
like a director
leading his
band. Music
is soft as soft
can be. Music
is like a rose
waking up.

Darlene Warren, *age 9*

Why should my ears
       hang down on music?
       The bird dances
Why couldn't I be music
       and fly?

                Timothy Dukes, *age 13*

MUSIC

Music is like a drum beating
harder and harder till it
breaks. Music is like a flower
tangling on the rainbow.
Music is like a person
standing some place
shivering cold.

                Carol Jones, *age 10*

SO WHAT'S THE PROBLEM WITH MAKING MUSIC?

A spoon or a bowl or two can make music.
A trumpet, a bass,
A loud voice that can break a vase,
That's music.
Bubble gum or a rake
Can make music.
A door, a roar, a snore
Make music.
So what's the problem
With making music?

                Robyn Stacy, *age 10*

Narrative

Telling a story in a poem might be an easy way to break away from the traditional forms and rhyming that some students have a tendency to imitate. There are possibilities in almost any kind of story material. Most students enjoy telling stories, from the little ones for whom fact and fiction are not too distinct, to the older ones who find it fun and an interesting challenge. If they have difficulty beginning, you could suggest that they choose a prose story they love and try putting it into narrative poetry. Perhaps you could use a picture of some people engaged in some activity. What is happening? What just happened? What is going to happen? Students will project their own moods and interpretations into any picture, and you will be surprised at the variety of poems you can get from the same picture.

A historical event that interests them may spark their imaginations. Something in the news might be written as a narrative poem. They might like writing a story about something that really happened in their lives, or something they wish had happened in their lives. Tall tales are fun, filled with exaggeration in the fashion of the American Tall Tales, told in a narrative poem. Science fiction is so popular in some places that a narrative poem on such a topic might be good. Tell a story backward, or make the impossible happen.

If the teacher-poet enjoys dramatization, try any kind of little pantomime which you think will bring a response, and ask the children to write a poem about it. If creative drama has been used previously, some members of the class might be willing to perform a short, spontaneous scene which could lead to poems. Keep the dramatization short. Discuss it before writing if it does not seem to be getting a fast response. If it looks like too weak an idea to use, forget it and try something else.

THE GIRL WHO WANTED A FLUTE

Once a girl wanted a new flute real bad
Her parents asked what was wrong
    with the one she had
She said it was just a toy
She didn't like it
Because it wouldn't make music.
So she began saving her money
Finally she saved enough
She didn't let her parents know,
She just went out in the meadow
And played her flute on a big rock.

        Connie Tate, *age 11*

A BLUE STORY

Because you put your blue hands on my blue coat
and opened the blue door
and walked up the blue steps
and held the blue rail
that led to the top of the blue steps
and walked to the blue door with the blue knob
and stepped into the blue room
beside the blue bed
and opened the blue chest
and got the BLUE INK
and put the blue ink all over me
and the floor
I am going to blue you
in the blue nose!

        Jeff Babb, *age 10*

BILLY C.

Billy C. was in love,
Till one day he got kissed.

Scott Mauney, *age* 10

Objects

A "thing" might make an easy topic with which to begin writing. Almost anything that is current and important in the life of the student could be used. A bike, chair, desk, bed, or a piece of sports equipment. For primary children, a toy, or for middle elementary a toy they used to have. Other things you could use are: a musical instrument, a clock, a good luck charm or a talisman, or a favorite item of clothing. It could be the family car or even the school bus. Consider using a religious object. A good way to motivate these poems might be telling about something that has or once had importance for you. There are many ways this idea can be explored. Speak of your use of the thing. Speak of your relationship to that thing. Do you love it? Do you hate it? Do you fear it? Maybe it is something you just wish you had. Why do you wish you had it? Personify the thing. Let it talk about its experiences and feelings.

AN AUTOMOBILE PERSON

Hello! My name is Baby.
I bet you think I'm a swinger
because of my name.
Not at all! I am an oldy as
some people call me.
I am much older than my
brother and sister.
I am the family's daughter's
car.

When people get in me I
hang down.
Some people call the outside of
me the body.
It is really my hair.
It used to be black.
Now it is white. I
am too old to be called BABY!

                Janice Carpenter, *age 10*

If I were a chair, I would yell when
        someone fat sat on me.
I would wish for someone skinny.
People don't have any consideration
        for chairs.
They always move me around and set
        books on my head.
They even write on me sometimes.
When I was born, I was just a piece
        of wood
        but I was formed into a chair.
I would like life a lot better if
        there were no such thing as fat
        people.

                Vanessa Dawn Vernon, *age 10*

CRYSTALS

Crystals are like glass.
Broken bits of glass
like broken bits of love.
Crystals are like people
always shaped differently.

You look at them and they
fade away.

Jill Stutzman, *age 10*

IF I WERE A THING

If I were a stove, I
wouldn't burn toast.

If I were a rubber band,
I'd pop my sister.

If I were a sink, I
wouldn't drip.

If I were a set of teeth,
I would bite my orthodontist.

If I were a light bulb, I
would never burn out.

If I were a garbage man,
I would hate trash.

If I were a shoe, I wouldn't
come untied.

If I were a wishing well,
I would make everyone's wishes come true.

Mary Craighill, *age 13*

MIRROR

In mirrors you can see yourself.
Some people look pretty and some
people look ugly. I like mirrors
because a mirror doesn't feel bad if
an ugly or a pretty person looks in it.

Teresa Williams, *age 10*

If I were a window
I would be open.
I wouldn't open like a door
or a water spigot,
or water draining out,
I would just be an odd thing.
I would be the only part of a
wall that goes up.
And if I were open
I could be hot or cold.

Terry Jones, *age 10*

Patriotism

This is one of the easiest subjects you can use, but because it has been used often in the schools, care must be taken to present the material in a fresh and honest way. Much patriotic writing is available as examples. This exercise could be especially effective if attempted in connection with the observance of some patriotic holiday. Focus on the flag or America. Good writing results if students are encouraged to express what America means to them and if you can carefully guide them away from the repetition of stale sentiments and cliches.

"Our flag is a great thing. When
a parade goes by with a person carrying
the flag, a sort of a chill runs through
your blood."

Jamie Severson, *age 10*

America! America!
Let the words upon the money
Show that they are true.

Linda Macdonald, *age 10*

America is all right I guess
Except for some things I see
Like one day I was on my way
To my grandmother's house
We passed this one corner
Which had a rotten apple half eaten
And a banana peel part black and yellow
A couple of cans rusty and empty
A couple of wine bottles
potato chips, corn chips, cookies, peanuts, popcorn wrappers
Left to rot
One day the people of America
Will get together
And clean up this mess.

                Julie Gabriel, *age 14*

AMERICA

I went down to a U.S.A. gas station last night
There was a giant American flag waving in the wind
I looked over the road
And saw cars and hundreds of people
And then I saw a plaque with this engraving:
This flag shall stay up day and night
Until every one of our P.O.W.'s is back home.
I feel good knowing I live in a country
That respects the right of every human being.
When I wake up
I know I am in America
And I am lucky.

                David Kitchens, *age 14*

People

This is a topic of universal interest and endless possibilities. Categories include people you know, friends, people you know about, people in a picture that is used as a shared experience, people in history or literature, people who are considered to be "different," and imaginary people. Describe them, compare them, explain them, or react to them. Someone in your family always makes a good topic.

MY PAPAW AND GRANDMAW

My papaw's about 73
And he still goes to work,
    feeds the dog, feeds the chickens
And he even goes swimming sometimes.
He always shows up
When he smells food.
He all the time fishes
At his cabin in the river.
We go fishing every weekend.

My grandmaw is 70 something.
She takes 10 pills every 6 hours
And she's not feeling good.
She always lays on the couch
Or walks out on the porch
And sets down.

They've been married 48 years.
My papaw goes to church every Sunday
And my family goes with him.
We've got movies of papaw dancing
When he was about 50.
I want to be like him

Because he's nice
And at his age he's still sprouting.

Marty Daniels, *age 11*

Someone you know to whom you are not emotionally tied makes an unimpassioned view possible. A neighbor or someone who used to be a neighbor might do. Teachers are not necessarily good subject matter, but if the students want to write about their teacher, don't forbid it. A sports hero might be interesting to write about, or an astronaut. People in history or literature make good subjects for poems. Tell about them. What made them great, greatly feared, or greatly disliked?

A friend can inspire a good poem. What is a friend? What is a perfect friend? Can you be a friend? The loss of a friend or why you need a friend can be the subject of poignant poems. How about writing about an imaginary friend? Primary grade children often have imaginary friends.

MY FRIEND

When I first met him, he hobbled on crutches.
A few years and he strengthened, but then,
    while rolling on skates, he broke his leg.
For a while he rode, I pushing,
Then for a few years he was
    nearly normal.
But then he rode again the hospital bed.
When he was back he limped badly.
Back to riding beds.
Now He Flies.

David Collins, *age 13*

Using a picture of a person or people works very well. Depending on the amount of experience the group has had, you might want to discuss the picture before you begin to write. What are the people doing? Why? What are they thinking? What kind of people are they? The "Family of Man" pictures have been used successfully. Describe the people. Tell what kind of lives you think they have. Be alert to the use of names of the individuals in the classroom so that this will not result in embarrassment.

A person who is considered to be "different" is a subject that has great potential. Why is he different? How is he different? Is he really different? Are we all different in some ways? You could use giants, dwarfs, people of different skin color, people who live in different communities and countries, and people who have different customs. A good introduction and discussion of "different" people could produce excellent poems by older children. Children younger than ten generally accept differences in people and do not consider them matters of consequence unless they have been taught to think otherwise.

PEOPLE

Some people are rich
Some people are poor
Some people have large families
Some people have small families
Some people burn coal heaters
Some people burn gas heaters
Some people live in slums
Some people live in nice houses
Some people eat meat and bread
Some people just eat bread
Some people dance rock 'n' roll
Some people dance square
Some people smell like soap
Some people smell like rats
All people can touch
All people can smell
All people can hear

All people can see
And all people can feel.

Donna McGill, *age 11*

People
Small, large
Moving, consuming, pretending.
Always on the move.
Humans.

Jamie Simms, *age 13*

Empathy develops when poems are written in which the student changes himself into the person about whom he is writing. Be that person. What bothers you? What makes you happy? What do you want to do? If you were a person in history or literature, how would you have behaved? Elementary children are enthusiastic about being imaginary people. Twelve-year-olds and older students can imagine themselves as increasingly complex and remote people who actually existed or exist.

EVERYBODY CAN WRITE

At age 25
    He has his sixth best seller
Harvard man.
        So what? Another one.
            Big Deal.

At age 62
    he writes his name for the first time
Just to sign his will
to leave his son all he owns
A knife, a shack, a blind dog!

Philip Pittman, *age 18*

Places

The poet-teacher and the students will be able to think of
many different kinds of places about which to write poems. Any
place that is special and interesting can be used as a topic for
poems.

> I do not know the name of the creek
> but I like to swim there and catch frogs.
> It is my little swimming hole
> because I put a NO TRESPASSING sign up.
> But I am thinking of taking it down.
> I caught a trout yesterday.
> I have my own cabin.
> Nobody lives there but me.
> It is fun being alone.
> You can do anything you want.
> I have turtle soup.
> I go hunting every day.
> I have twenty hunting dogs.
> I will get along.
>
> Mike Peake, *age 7*

Use home, the student's room at home, a favorite place, a "secret" place, a vacation, or an entertainment place.

> THE LOFT IN RAIN
>
> Up here, a palace.
> Alone completely.
> The loft, untouched except for me!
> A kingdom
> dusty, sweet, prickly hay
> yellow grass

rain going thumpety-thump
a tin roof, very thin
thumpety-thump
Light? Where is it?
Behind a door
cool air and a meadow
pools and puddles, thumpety-thump
the reflection of the sky
birds cloud the reflection
gone in a screech and rush of wings
door closed
darkness thumpety-thump
a collection of wine bottles
green, dusty, old, leering
big and fat
tiny ones, green, red, blue
dusty and small
a chair and table, dusty
holding memories
also dusty
a teacup, old and worn
chipped and no handle
smashing spiders
night comes, slowly
creeping up
touching me and my kingdom.
Submit.
Until tomorrow.
I will come again.

Sarah Hewson, *age 15*

A foreign country could be used, perhaps one that the class has studied.

ETHIOPIA

Ethiopia—a strange
and interesting land
Where all people seem
happy and contented.

Ethiopia—a land of
Two mile high
Mountains above
Dry, barren deserts.

Ethiopia—a land with
A three thousand year
History as colorful
And varied as its people.

Ethiopia—a land of
High rises and muddy
Roads, a land of daily
Open air markets and
Peasants with burros.

Dargan Moore, *age 14*

The teacher-poet or the students can draw a map of an imaginary place and write about it. What kind of place is it? Is it a perfect place? Is it some future place?

One useful device to introduce places is to have a "looking window." If the room in which you are working is constructed with one or more large windows that command a view, you can use the windows. The window frame is like a picture frame, and through the glass you have a living picture. Describe the view; compare the view; give your personal reactions to the view. You are fortunate if you find a window through which you can see things that are seasonal like trees or other plantings, or people going about their business. If you are using a place other than the one you can see through the looking window, you could write the poems as if you were there.

LOOKING WINDOW

The fifth grade has a looking window. Each day we look out the window and see how many things are turning green. All around the school things are turning green and yellow and they look so pretty. When you look out the window you can see a big tree that fell down during the winter, and now there are little insects and other things living in it.

We decided to turn our desks toward the window so now we can all see through the window from our desks. We can all see the world awaken.

Timmy Muldowney, *age 10*

Poetry—poets

Another idea that can produce interesting poems is, what is a poem, or what is poetry? This topic would be best used after a poet's visit, or after the students have had some good experiences in writing as well as in hearing and reading poems. If there is to be a poet available for readings or to spend some time in residence, it is interesting for students to speculate about what it will be like to have a poet in school. What will it be like to have a poet for a teacher? What kind of person do you think a poet is? After the poet's visit, or as a last topic during the residence, poems could be written about what it was actually like to read and write poems.

SOME ANSWERS TO FOUR QUESTIONS

What is a poem?

"A poem is when you uncan all the imagination inside you."
"A poem is a feeling that yearns for someone to hear."

"Poems are works of art that can be written by anybody."
"A poem is a gathering of many or one."

What is a poet?

A poet is a person who makes a sad person happy,
an old person feel young again
a lonely person feel surrounded with friends.

What will it be like to have a poet at school?

"The poet will tell you what a poem is like and then go away."
"It will be exciting because I've never seen a poet."
"It will be like books, but better."
"It will be like feeling popular."

What was it really like to have a poet?

"It was like having thousands of thoughts pop up in the air and get drawn down by pencils."
"I thought it would be fun, but not this fun. It made me feel wanted."
"There was nothing between us but floor and air."
"It was a time when we laughed and thought of many things, true and false."

Jo Hassett's Fifth Grade Class

Protest

Protest is a topic especially captivating for young people offended by hypocrisy, pollution, war, social and racial inequities, and corruption.

HENRY'S FATHER

As a child I liked Henry's father
Towering above me he seemed as huge
As Paul Bunyan, I guess all men
Seem that way when you're small.

My parents and their friends
Said he was a very nice man.
When he died from a hunting accident
My parents and their friends
Said he was a great man.

I was young
And I didn't understand death,
But I learned one thing
From Henry's father's death:
One has to die
To achieve greatness.

                    Andrea Jones, *age 14*

THE DEBUTANTE

With proper smiles on painted faces,
White satins, silks and imported laces
Bought only at a certain store,
Grace only the best young girls on the floor.
Each mother, aware of her fading beauty,
Whispers to her daughter that it is her duty
To waltz with her father and bow to the town,
And, for the family's name, to put the cigarette down.
The picture in the paper and the final ball
Display the wealth and society for all.

On the girls, the white gowns look so pure,
But of the girls, the parents are not so sure.

                    Carson Dowd, *age 17*

WHERE, WHY, WHAT

But where did young Charles go
        Boys, oh where has he gone?
        He's gone away to another world
        gone away never to return.

But why did he leave us
    Boys, oh why did he go?
    He left 'cause they told him so
    And what they say goes.

But what gives them the right
    Boys, oh what gives them the right?
    They're the leaders of our nation
    Although they lead us without sight.

But what can we do
    Boys, oh what can we do?
    There's nothing left for you son,
    Just get ready to carry a gun.

        Harold Howe, *age 18*

I WONDER WHY

I wonder why the skies are not blue
        anymore,
I wonder why the lakes do not feed fish
        anymore,
I wonder why the fields there were are
        no more,
I know why, because we did not wonder
        more.

        Read Tull, *age 14*

THE GREAT SPELL

People cough and scream.
In colonial days people
Stole Indians' land and sold people.
Now we pollute and kill and hurt and steal.
It is all terrible.

I'll change it!
World, start over.
Turn a new leaf over.
Begin again now.

We will not make mistakes.
Breathe deeply.
See how clean the air is now.
We have no guns to kill with
Or diseases.
Animals are our friends,
Even lions and tigers
Are friendly.
There is no overpopulation.

Everything is trouble-free,
As long as I can hold this spell.
Until
Now.

Katie Dagenhart, *age 10*

Rhythm

Walking or writing within a suggested rhythm is not only fun,
it is easy. Ask children to think of their favorite song and say or
write new words for it. Or establish a simple rhythm on drums
or by clapping hands. It is easy to swing into the beat and add
words. Rhyming seems natural to this exercise, and nonsense
often occurs. Young poets should be encouraged to develop their
rhythms and also make sense in the poems.

I can't wait to Thanksgiving morn
A big fat turkey and lots of corn
I'll eat and I'll eat 'till there is no more
I'll look at football 'till my eyes are sore.

Tony Fewell, *age 11*

SUN AND THE MOON

Sun came up and the moon went down
And the people went to work
Ladies gossiping
Men talking business
Boys looking at girls
Sun went down, moon came up
Ladies and men going out
Boys and girls going on dates
That's what happens in the night
    and day.

        Lynn Mauney, *age 12*

THE DRUM POEM

I can't wait till Christmas comes
Then I'll dance and play these drums
Santa Claus will be the best
I can't get a night of rest
Thinking about my 10 speed bike
Nothing be wrong, things will be right
When I get out on the street
I'll wave to everyone I meet

        Gary Avery, *age 10*
        James Avery, *age 11*
        Marty Daniels, *age 11*

MEAT SANDWICH POEM

Went up to a man one day
Asked for 50 cents to pay
For a hamburger with cheese.
Give it to me Mister, please.

He said I ain't got the dough
So I thought that I would go
Around the corner to my house
And make a sandwich of a mouse.

Gary Avery, *age 10*
James Avery, *age 11*
Marty Daniels, *age 11*

An old-timey dune buggy goes
pop bang crackle
boom bam whoop
bam crackle pop
bong pop whoop
pop crackle bam boom tub
tuk tuk   tuk tuk
tuk   tuk   tuk
. . . . tuk.

Keith Barnes, *age 8*

Religion

Religion is an important subject for poems. Choose from the entire gamut of religions in humankind's history and live religions all over the world today. The student's personal religious beliefs or experiences, agnosticism, or atheism could produce good poems in high school. God, the meaning of life, prayer, heaven, death, life after death, Indian ceremonials, Christian sacraments, or any other rites which have meaning for the group could be used. Don't forget voodooism, witchcraft, or other local sorcery.

GOD

I've always wondered how God came to be.
Who borned him or what started him?

I've wondered about that all my life.
I also wonder
Why doesn't God come to Earth in person
So we would know it was Him?

Margaret Storrs, *age 10*

With the passing of a life, the oldest clean soul
Can if it wants to,
Enter the world as a new born child.
If not, however,
The possibility passes to the next
Youngest of the souls,
To the next
To the next
Dot. Dot. Dot.

Anonymous, *age 15*

CAIN

He is sitting there upon that rock watching, waiting.
He has seen the empty shells of man dressed in deep
Purple and rich black lying in caskets of dark mahogany.
He has seen the lips of the paste colored faces turned down
In flat, smooth frowns.
He has watched the invisible shadows' ascent for
millions of
Years and yet he will never go.
He will remain forever upon that rock watching, waiting
for his time to come, but it never shall, for he is Cain.

Catherine Mesrobian, *age 16*

Science Fiction

This topic is not as appealing to children as it would seem at
first. They seem to use their imaginations better when they be-

gin with topics with which they have had some experience. However, space fantasy is fascinating to some and these children can become enthusiastic when telling about flying saucers, the creatures who inhabit other planets. Older students can imagine and plan systems of social structure which are different and often improve upon the governments and life styles on earth.

THE THING

There it was!
A monster.
Red and blue,
Smelled like a swamp.
Walking on one leg,
Rough and scaly,
Spraying saliva all over.
A square and a blob,
Matted hair,
Purple eyes,
Against the horizon
Huge, dangerous, savage,
Galloping, creeping, swimming
Screaming—
Monster!

Marion Hanes, *age 12*

SPACE FANTASY

I hear a spaceship
landing.
I am hiding behind
an orange hill.
The alien creatures have
six green eyes.
They are coming;

They talk like crows.
When I talk
I hear an echo.
They got me now.

David Hill, *age 13*

A GOOMIE-GOOMIE OR A GOONIE-GOONIE

It was a strange day
I decided to stop and play at a
    near-by playground.
I was playing on the monkey bars.
All of a sudden all the people
    in the park disappeared.
When I started to go home
A bunch of little furry things
That were red, yellow, light green,
    and purple
Jumped out from behind the trees.
I made friends with them
(I had no other choice)
They were very nice after all.
Now all of them are dead except two.
1 Goomie-Goomie and 1 Goonie-Goonie.
I will give a reward of 10 dollars
    to the person or thing that
    happens to find one.

Anonymous, *age 11*

Senses

Paying attention to sense experiences and relating them in words is a good exercise in increasing awareness. It can result in good poems. The suggestions for writing a collaboration poem contain information on the use of the senses. Sense experiences enrich poems written on any topic, and some poems rely primarily on the expression of sense images.

AN APPLE

An apple looks like a white ball
That fell into red paint.
An apple smells like seaweed
An apple tastes like cinnamon
An apple feels like a little pumpkin
Or a big cherry.
An apple sounds like potato chips
When you bite.
Crunch, crack, crunch.

Collaboration poem, *6 and 7 year old children*

Smells

For high school students, incense can be used as a subject for poems and also to create a special atmosphere in the room. Spray cans of room freshener in various scents are useful to stimulate poems and have an advantage since they dissipate quickly.

Fragrant herbs can be used. If it is a small group, carry the herbs around and let the students take turns smelling them. If you can get a large enough supply, pass around a small quantity to each student. Be prepared to discover that some students will say some odors you enjoy are unpleasant to them. Various perfumes and colognes seem to evoke strongly agreeable or strongly disagreeable sensations in different people. It does not work well to use something which you know is generally considered to be an unpleasant scent.

A RAIN OF FLOWERS

The floral spray makes the room smell like
A candle shop or green house.

It smells like some teachers sometimes.
It smells like a pear tastes.
It makes me feel a happy dizziness like I feel
Going to a dance in a pink polka-dot dress
Or like when Gwen's soft laughing makes me laugh.
It makes me think of
My mother's linen closet,
Sleeping under a baby's blanket
Or walking in a rain of flowers.

Collaboration poem, *12 year olds*

SMELLS

Bacon smells like a kitchen
Flowers smell like peaches
A skunk smells like pollution
Something old smells like a dirty bed
Both my feet smell like each other
Lemons are like perfume
My mother smells like my hands.

Collaboration poem, *7 year olds*

Sounds

Poems can be written about any kind of sound you can create.
Records are available which reproduce sounds of the city streets,
sirens, fireworks, harbor sounds, shrieks, creaking doors, and a
great variety of other sounds. You can bring a bell into the classroom and ask for comparison poems. The bell sounds like . . .
If the school bell rings while your group is in session, that could
be used to evoke ideas. You can try a small drum, the sound
of paper being torn or crackled, an electric razor, an egg beater,
or tapping a pencil on a desk. Bring in a music box, produce
sounds on a musical instrument, or use music on records.

SOUNDS

All the girls in my class go yapetee,
　　yapetee, yapetee, most of the time.
Last night I heard the crickets go
　　cricket-cricket.
And the frogs went grumpet-grumpet.
When I get up in the morning I hear
　　birds go tweet-tweet.
And I heard my next door guinea-pigs
　　go skeak-skeak.

　　　　　Mark Hinshaw, *age 9*

THE FAT MAN

There was a man who always said ugg ugg.
There was another man who said he he.
There was a woman who said how how.
And another one said shu shu.
And another one said ha ha.
And they got together and made a band.
It sounded
　　ugg ugg
　　he he
　　how how
　　shu shu
　　ha ha
　　　over and over.

　　　　　Mark Hartsell, *age 11*

The frog sounds like a light-
house horn in the fog guiding
ships to land.

　　　　　Bruce White, *age 12*

Sights

This sense can be used reflectively as in a description, or given imaginary treatment. Say what something looks like, but what it really is. Pictures that you flash to the class, or pictures that remain stationary for them to refer to as they write are stimulating. Good imaginary poems can result when you ask the students to tell what they see with their magic eye, the one that is inside of their heads and is only open when their two regular ones are closed.

SIGHTS

Down on the pond I have
seen many beautiful things:
a fluffy swan, the shiny water,
and many red roses. I have seen
a dead tree, a tree that had
pretty colored leaves, and a
tree with a hole in it. Many
pretty things to see . . . and a
little duck in the water, too.

Dave Foltz, *age 10*

Tastes

This sense is difficult to use in the classroom because it can so easily lead to unpleasant gastronomic references. Pass out mints or other small candies and have students tell about the taste. Ask them to recall something good they have eaten, and write a poem about that. With older students you might describe a gourmet meal and have them write how they imagine it would taste.

My name is Deborah
I like for breakfast
Egg, bacon, orange juice
For lunch I like
Hot dogs and French fries
I don't care too much
    about supper.

          Deborah Dreher, *age 11*

Touch

If you can provide something for each student to touch, this will set off good poems. Anything from bits of sandpaper to pieces of velvet or fur will do. The degree of texture will affect the vividness of expression. If you decide to use this sense on the spur of the moment and have not provided materials to be touched, suggest that they touch the textures of something they are wearing, or their hair, a book, paper, or the desk. Older students might be able to write about touch experiences from their memories.

      WHAT IS IN THE BAG?

A toy with hair
It feels like a rabbit,
A koala bear,
A ball of fur,
A rat with no tail.
I think it has big eyes.
It feels all fuzzy and warm.
What can it be?
PLEASE let us see.

          Collaboration poem, *age 6*

Movement

This topic requires space if it is to be immediate-experience related. Younger children can swing on the swing, use the teeter-totter, slide on the slide, run, skip, or do whatever they do at play, and then tell you how it felt. If you can use a large empty room, elementary children could move to music or beats of a drum and write about it. You could turn to imaginary movement and ask them how it would feel to fly if they were birds, swim if they were fish, or lumber through the jungle if they were elephants! Find out what motion experiences the older children enjoy, such as running, skating, skiing, riding in an open vehicle, or engaging in some sports activity. Ask them to write about it. How do you move? How does it feel?

SKATING

I love to go skating
In my own white skates
It makes me feel like I'm riding on air
It makes me feel like I'm being myself
And nobody else.
When I'm moving fast
I feel like I'm free
Like I'm flying around
Up and down and around
I love to go skating
In my own white skates
Because it makes me feel like me.

Wanda Lanier, *age 13*

HONDA

The wind, as it gushes across my face, stings like a thousand prickling needles . . . I'm past the bridge and flying up the

135 degree angle of the hill. When I reach the top, I feel
like I'm on the top of the world as I look down at the scat-
tered houses and the creek at the bottom of the slope . . .
The next jump is fast approaching and I prepare first by
slowing down. More gas, more speed, takeoff, soar, touchdown, conquest. I head for the creek to feel the spray as I
charge through, over the bridge, flying over the jumps and
charging.

Sam Deal, age 13

Silence

What do you hear when you hear silence? Even the contradic-
tion in that question could be the subject of a poem. Ask the
group to try to be perfectly still and write poems about what they
hear. Ask them to listen for something specific in the silence.
Can they hear noises in their heads? Can they hear themselves
think? Can they remember a time when it actually was silent?
How do they feel about silence? Do they sometimes wish for
it? What would it be like to be deaf? How would you write a
silent poem?

ALONE IN THE PARK

Being alone in the park
with your dog,
Meditating alone
by yourself,
Listening to the
leaves blow
and children scream,
watching people
go by,
feeling that feeling
of aloneness.

John Belk, age 12

PEACE IS . . .

Peace is harmony,
silence, calm,
repose, rest.
Peace is the happy,
natural state of man.
It is his birthright.
War is his disgrace.

Peace is a state of quiet,
A freedom from disturbance,
anxiety, agitation,
riot or violence,
God is peace!

Craig Hill, *age 13*

QUIETNESS

The nature I see
is a green tree
or a squirrel staring at me.
But what I hear
is like seeing with my ear
it is like the wilderness awaiting me.
I hear the birds singing
the wind humming
even the river running.
Quietness
is what I want.

Libby Crist, *age 10*

Sports

All children have been exposed to sports in one way or another and most of them have played competitive or team sports. Many children enjoy competitive sports at school or have favorite professional teams in baseball, football, hockey. Individual sports like swimming and golf also become interesting topics for poems if you discuss the possibilities of poetry revealing why the student prefers one sport to another, what feelings he has while watching or participating, what makes each sport unique.

VOLLEYBALL

I feel like I can jump to the sky
When I play volleyball. It is like
Hitting the moon with all my might.
The net in between is the sky
I knock the moon to another part of the world
When it is night
I have hit the moon
Far away.

Sharon Ryars, *age 13*

EYES OF A FULLBACK

In the huddle
And they call your number
You know it's your time to run the ball
You start getting nerves
You start getting ready by the time he says hut
You are more than ready
You run through the line
Like running through a wall
You run hard
You try not to fall
You look around
And you don't even have the ball
It is on the ground
You run back

You have the ball
You run for daylight
But you get hit
You spin away
You run across the goal line
But you went the wrong way
Instead of your team getting the touchdown
The other team wins the game.

Jeff Wortman, *age 14*

Time

What is time? What does it feel like at different times of the day, at different times in your life? Why are clocks important? Are they important to everyone? Do you think you would sense what the time is if you did not have a clock? Is the time of year important to you? If you lived in a climate where seasons did not change or the nights were very long, how would this affect your sense of time?

SOME TIMES

Ding makes me feel
like I am at church
Dong makes me feel
like I am in London.

Lisa Bunch, *age 10*

THE CLOCK

The clock ticks away
Second by second
Minute by minute

Hour by hour
Week by week
Month by month
Year by year
It flies by so fast
You don't think you'll last
Everything seems to be lost
in the past.

Anonymous, *age 15*

LIFE

As I think of what my life has been,
Just a whisper of time
It brings tears to my eyes
To think I won't be here much longer.
Millions upon millions of years
go by but are only a speck in God's eye.

Robert Mason, *age 12*

Travel

The idea of travel is akin to the idea of escape, and contains an element of adventure. The travel experience itself makes a good topic for poems. How can you travel in your poem? Starting with your feet, you can go to bicycles, motorbikes, cars, trains, airplanes, jets, rockets to the moon, flying balloons, helicopters, hovercraft, cable cars, trains, boats of various kinds, water skis, horseback, UFO's, and Magic Flying Carpets! Invent a new way to travel. How will we travel in the future? If you want to go in the other direction in time, write a poem about some historical means of travel such as covered wagons, or carriages. This can be adapted to any age.

AN OCEAN TRIP

I'm on a ship to West Africa
and I am listening
to a world of water.
The sea gulls sound like squeaking doors.
Waves sound like glasses
falling on the floor.
The sun's rays hit with hotness
and make me feel like I'm stranded.

Andy Whitson, *age 10*

THE MOON

Take a trip to the moon sometime in June,
Take off in a big rocket
And maybe the conductor will let you dock it.
With your space suit on and your tanks
Full of oxygen, take an ounce or two
It would be nifty to step fifty feet high
Way up in the sky.

Dewey Dorsett, *age 10*

AIRPLANE TRIP

An airplane is smoother than a car
In a car you can't play chess or checkers
A 747 is big
You can play a game of magnetic checkers
On the plane
You can listen to music,
Watch movies,
Play cards.

I like the take-off and landing best.
My mother likes landings.
She knows she's back on the ground.

Ken Martin, *age 12*

A SUBWAY RIDE

Once I was on a subway.
It was dark and dim.
When you sat down in your seat
You felt as if you didn't weigh much.
There were some stumps on the track.
When the train went over them
You went up in the air like a bird.
At the end of the trip
You came out of the pipe.

Karen Roboz, *age 10*

Trees

Because children love nature, they love to talk and write about
animals and plants and trees. The imaginations of young children are caught by wondering what plants and trees might say
if they could talk, or by describing their favorite tree and telling
why they love it. Special trees, a Christmas tree fully decorated
or discarded, a certain tree near the school or in the park, make
good topics.

THE TREE

Oh, big tree,
I am sorry that your branch is broken.
You look like a dragon with sparkling
   flames.

Your designs are so beautiful,
I can almost see them sparkling in the sun
I can almost see you move and turn.

Nobel Olson, *age 11*

Pine trees hide many
Secrets. They will not
Tell us. They whisper
At night.

Mike Junior, *age 14*

The Universe

The whole planet earth, volcanoes, mountains, glaciers, deserts, oceans, rivers, streams, lakes, ponds, even puddles can be subjects for talking and writing. Stars, planets, or other kinds of worlds imagined to exist are possibilities. If you do not start with a walk, think of an exciting way to introduce the topic you choose in order to capture the imagination of the group. Consider poems relating to something studied in geography. Tell why the topic interests you. Ask for the students' thoughts, ideas, or questions about the universe.

STARS

Stars sometimes
    Give me a gloomy feeling
        And sometimes not.
This is how I think of the stars.
I think of them as little
        Bits of sand,
    And sometimes tears.
How do you think of the stars?

Mary Margaret Carter, *age 8*

SUN

The sun sinks into
Clear blue water like an orange,
Until nothing is left except the
Seeds shooting outward.

Jeff Burnette, *age 14*

Values–Human and Moral

From the Holy Scriptures and McGuffey's Readers to present-day organizations which fight prejudice, there is a wealth of material available for use in the consideration of human values and morals. With primary children, remember to use experience-oriented poems. Sharing toys, playing with one another fairly, and name-calling may be suggested by them as matters of concern.

Many of the ideas listed under "people" can be oriented to discussion of strengths and weaknesses of character. Current events topics can be evaluated in terms of the absence or presence of moral values. It is possible that the morality of certain activities engaged in or observed by the group will interest them as topics. The morality of humankind in relation to the planet and other people is a deep concern for older students. History offers opportunities for moral evaluations. Literature which has been shared by the group can become the topic of poems on human and moral values. Sometimes a TV show or movie that most of them have seen can be used. Scientific research has moral implications. The topic of euthanasia might interest some high school seniors. A changing sense of values could be discussed and explored in poems.

A TRICK

When you work, work carefully,
So you won't get it wrong.

When you sleep, sleep quietly,
But don't sleep too long.

When you eat, eat carefully,
So you will not get sick.

Doing things carefully,
Is a handy trick.

Kathy Severson, *age 10*

OLD PEOPLE

Worn out bodies
Wrinkled and frail,
Gray hair,
No hair,
Still have fun in their own way.
Watching T.V.
Seeing children,
Or just reading a letter.
In hospitals,
In institutions,
In centers,
Old people,
Useless,
Dying,
Loved.

Lance Stokes, *age 11*

TIME

Peace is like time
You've gotta have both to have both.

Nancy Murray, *age 15*

And though we try, we don't know why
We live to love and love to hate.

                    Cindy Nisbet, *age 14*

A walk

The place in which we live is a source of wonder and interest
for all ages. A shared experience might be a walk in the woods,
a park near the school, the community of homes, city streets, or
a factory district. If you are going to take a walk, prepare the
children. Tell them that they are going to look and listen. You
might want to ask what they expect to see. What colors will there
be? When they say green, ask if they think everything will be
the same kind of green. What other colors will they see? Will
the colors look the same in the sun as in the shade? How will
they be different? What other things will you see? How big or
how little will the things be? What textures will you see or feel?
If the students do not suggest that they will hear something, ask
them what they think they might hear. Ask them if they think
everything will be still or if things will be moving. Will we see
everything that there is to see?

If the students are old enough to jot down things they observe, they might take their notebooks and pencils. You can use
the material gathered to write a collaboration poem if this group
has not had enough experience to write individually. If the
group has not been responding richly, you might want to spend
a little time asking individuals to read some of their ideas or tell
you about something they saw or heard. Sometimes if you do
this before the quiet writing time begins, it is a help to those
who are not as receptive and responsive.

A WALK IN THE CITY

Cars, people, trucks, sirens
but if you listen you can hear

two birds calling to each other
across a space made by bulldozers
you can feel the air in your hair
you can think about how people
and the earth were made.
The dust rises in the park
and nuts bounce on the pavement
like rubber balls.

Collaboration poem, *ages 10 and 11*

A WALK IN THE COUNTRY

Some trees reach up
and some hang down.
I saw an ant swim in an acorn shell
and a grasshopper hide.
It looks and sounds like things are dead
but you know they are alive.
The vines look like they are trying
to strangle each other.
The trees are struggling with the wind.
The trees don't move at the same time
and it makes you feel like the ocean
is there in the woods.

Collaboration poem, *ages 10 and 11*

Weather

Should any interesting weather be happening, use it! Turn off
the lights, open the windows, or go outside. Look at it, listen to
it, feel it! You can use everything from a small breeze to a hurri-
cane. If you can get films or pictures about weather, or share the
memory of a recent storm, it helps to evoke strong poems. Any
kind of precipitation, snow, rain, hail can be used. The way the

world looks just after rain or snow is good too. Primary children can have fun with interesting clouds. If there is a place where they can lie on the ground and look up, make cloud pictures into poems.

NANTUCKET, MASS.

The wind starts to blow
Howling, screaming
It makes the waves
Bounce into shore,
Higher, higher, crashing,
Rolling, plunging, breaking.
The rain begins to fall.
Gently at first, then
Harder, harder,
Bouncing into the surf.
Water rises higher.
Lightning flashes
Thunder roars
suddenly ending with a
great crash it all stops.
Gently the waves roll by.

Lu Kelly, *age 13*

The rain comes down
Drip, drop, drip,
And waters the town
So we don't have to.

Shelly Boulware, *age 7*

The snow grew thick on the bare ground
The wind blew the branches all around

The white flakes fell, hiding the sun
They were all different, every one.

> Alice Kern, *age 12*

Raindrops beat against the windowpane,
Gently at first, then harder—
Making designs as they fall,
Much the same as across a tear-stained face.
I look out on the world
    through this blurred vision,
And wonder why things are
    the way they are,
While it continues to rain
Gently at first, then harder.

> Merrin Sweeney, *age 17*

SPRING SPRINKLE

The sun is shining bright,
The trees are swaying.
The fields have a golden shine.
A sprinkle comes up.
Now the fields have a silver shine
Only half of the sun is showing.
A breeze is swaying the grain.
The dirt is moving.

> Joe B., *age 8*

This is the wind,
    a dog running through leaves,
    a dog howling at the moon.

> Sandi Vestal, *age 12*

FOG

The fog comes here
And then goes there,
What do you think it is?
The fog is just
A little cloud
That lowered itself to here.

Priss Justis, *age 10*

Wishes

There is special magic in wishes. The experience of wishing
is common to everyone, and writing poems about it is easy and
fun. It might be a good beginning experience with poetry. Let
your imagination loose. Wishes can take the form of prayers, in-
cantations, or spells. With the younger children who have heard
or read fairy tales, you might suggest that they make three wishes.
Any age would enjoy wishing they had certain powers that human beings don't have. Suggest using language powerful enough
to ensure that the wishes will come true. This is a topic that could
be approached successfully even in high school. What do you
wish you could do? What do you wish you had? How do you
wish you could change the world?

THE KING OF THE WORLD

I wish I were the king of the world
So I would not have to take a bath
And I could eat all the food in the world
And I would drink all the milk in the world
I'm going to live in a gold house
I will make the sun shine 100 hours a day
And I get paid 1 cent

After 1,000,000,000,000 years
I would take a bath
In a swimming pool.

        Timothy Bilbrey, *age 12*

I wish I were a star far,
        far up in the sky.
And every night I could twight,
        twight all night long.
And every child would say
        look at that star twight.

        Patricia Morgan, *age 11*

I wish I were a kitten as soft as silk,
I wish I could drink milk from a saucer.
I wish I were gray as smoke from the fire
        with eyes as blue as the sky.
I wish people with soft warm hands
        would pat me.

        Jana Callicutt, *age 9*

I wish the clouds would all turn
        green so it would snow frogs.
I wish our house was made of sticks.
I wish it would snow goats so I
        could get my garbage up.

        Greg Abernathy, *age 10*

I wish I had a pink arched,
birch-bark mobile,

the color of pink
from a spray can, of course,
no wheels, only lady bugs
sprayed pink
with a cover of maple leaves
for when it rains
sprayed pink, of course,
and as it goes
it plays selections from Bach
and beeps like a road-runner
sprayed pink, of course.

Jill Stutzman, *age 10*

Wonder, Mystery, Miracles, and Magic

Students are full of unanswered questions, so a poem about wondering is a natural. What do you wonder about? Wonder what would happen if . . . ? If I were the last leaf on the tree . . . If I were the last person on earth . . . I wonder why?

Mystery ideas can go off in many directions. For the older students, use any of the mysteries of life, death, earth, universe, or eternity. The topics mentioned under the heading of religion can be approached as mysteries. Some things are called "spooky" by younger children. Most groups would enjoy writing ghost poems. Try this: If I could make myself invisible, I would . . . Anything seen by the student-poet as a miracle can be used. Try the word "magic" and see what happens. If you were a magician, what magic would you want to do? The older children might be intrigued by writing about a mystery in their lives. Motivation for the writing could be supplied by relating a source of wonder or mystery in the life of the teacher-poet.

MY WONDERS

I wondered, at two years old,
    if the sky would ever
    fall in.

I wondered, at four years old,
  if I would ever fall
  off my bike.
I wondered, at six years old,
  if I would be a
  fireman or a doctor.
I wondered, at eight years old,
  if school would be
  fun (or hard).
I wondered, at ten years old
  if my brother and I
  would ever dislike the
  sport of killing each other.
I wondered, at twelve years old,
  what it would be like
  becoming a teenager.
I wondered, at fourteen years old,
  what other wonders
  I would have in the future.

Gus Clark, *age 14*

BLACK MAGIC

Monheeny, quazinny, zickety-zam!
The moon will crash with a great big bam!
The sun will explode, the stars will reverse,
I will destroy the wide Universe!
The heavens collapse, the planets will fall,
When I am through, there will be nothing at all.
Not a thing will exist, not even a horse.
Everything will be gone, except me, of course.

Mark Culton, *age 11*

A MURDER SPELL

A dash of swamp toe tail,
A dash of turtle ears,
A dash of warlock wart,
A dash of tadpole's eye,
Last of all, a human heart,
You have the mixture to corrode the world,
You can burn up a snake
You can turn the universe red.

Paul Warley, *age* 10

A MYSTERY

From nowhere a lion smiled
To comfort our confusion of illusions
And show us a silver starshine cowboy . . .
Long time gone.
Here I am again a lonely mustang
Living black and white
Remembering the night the lion smiled.

Anonymous, *age* 13

Work

The kinds of work, the importance of work, the interests in a certain work, are topics that attract many children. There are many questions which might make this topic interesting; is work necessary for everyone, what are the most interesting jobs, how much do you think people should work, what does work mean to the individual, to the society? This exercise can increase capacity for observing details and lead into many philosophical ideas.

WORK

The young men work
And they greet the work with laughter and they seldom think
Of the work that follows after, and they fight and drink
Just like comrades all together
And the old men shiver when the wind blows cold.

The bright, strong men
Who can use their heads for thinking might as well lay bricks
On the foundations that are sinking, for the house they'll build
Will be just like every other when the wind blows cold.

Jeff Wright, *age 15*

MY WORK

I do the dishes
It dulls my mind
And nobody ever says,
"Your dishwashing is lovely."

Debbie Bober, *age 10*

WORK

The drone of the vacuum cleaner,
The swish of the duster,
Or of the mop,
The scraping of this pencil,
And deep inside your body
The thump of your heart
Are sounds of something working.

Jeannie Snow, *age 10*

It is almost impossible to write freely when rhyme and form are stressed. It is more important to unleash imagination and enthusiasm for language than it is to teach forms and terminology. Students who have had an overdose of poetics and are inhibited about trying something more free might be reminded that styles in poetry change just like dress styles, that styles and the vocabulary of one hundred years ago are not an adequate expression for today's life styles.

Poetry might be defined as imaginative language that sometimes has patterns. These patterns need not be patterns of rhyme but can be patterns evolved from the subject, the mood, the idea in the writing.

WHO ARE YOU?

I am Leslie Strawn sitting in a creative writing class.
No, now I am eyes watching a simple bug crawl up the wall.
Is he as simple as he seems?
Now I am ears listening to a bird chirp and another bird
    answer
No, now I am a dream floating in a cloud.
"Leslie, you are not writing!"
I am Leslie Strawn sitting in a creative writing class.

Leslie Strawn, *age 10*

MY NAME IS DEBBIE

I don't like my legs but I like to run
I like my arms but I don't like to slap
I like my eyes but I don't like the way they're made
I like my mouth but I don't like to brag.

Debbie Hoover, *age 10*

To write a poem takes:
   spelling,
   grammar,
   ideas
And most of all it takes:
   a mean
   lowdown
   English teacher.
So I can't write a poem.

       Anonymous, *age 14*

T he most important person
O ther than my mother is
M e, TOM

   age 12

Of course rhythm and rhyme have a place in the language of
poetry. Patterns add music and make words more memorable.
The littlest children sometimes insist on making their poems
move in some rhythm they can feel in their bodies. Everyone
loves riddles and the humor that can evolve from rhyming.

   FACES

Some faces are old and frail
Some faces look white and pale
Some have dimples
Some have pimples
Some are fair
Some have hair
Each has a nose
Not one has toes.

     Patti, Leslie, and Julie, *age 11*

I have a pony
Named Macaroni
Believe it or not
This poem is baloney.

Tommie Price, *age* 7

When opportunity for creativity is given, children need to be reassured that what they have to say is more important than the form of the words. With continued experience in talking, hearing, reading, and writing poems, older children will begin to adopt patterns as they are ready for them and become interested. If specific patterns are not taught, the young writers will frequently invent their own. If freedom of expression has already been experienced, older students might like to discuss the following simple forms and perhaps try them as an exercise for fun with language.

The Collaboration Poem

Writing a collaboration poem is a useful way to get students started writing their own poems. Procedures and types of poems will vary according to the age of the class and the inclinations of the teacher-poet. Subjects will also vary, but will usually succeed best if related to immediate experience shared by the group. For instance, writing a poem about a live animal which children can see and touch will produce better poetry than just telling the class to write about an animal. Writing about a flower which they can see and possibly smell will produce better poems than writing about "flowers." The younger the students, the more "deprived" they are, or the less experience they have had in creative expression, the more necessary it is to supply the shared experience. Also, actual things succeed better than representations of things. Pictures, films, and slides succeed better with pupils who are more mature and able to make the transition from the abstract to their own experience.

Some poet-teachers enjoy choosing an imagined idea for a collaboration poem. Examples of this are: If I were an elephant, I would . . . , or themes relating to unusual treatment of color or sound. This is harder to do than the direct experience for a first collaboration, and might give disappointing results. With upper elementary children, abstractions are more productive after you know the class and have some ideas that you feel would interest them. The very youngest might have imaginations free enough to make up *anything!* The older students, especially high school, might feel safer at first with impersonal devices than with anything that would reveal their own ideas and emotions. Wordplay, concrete poetry, take five, or some other impersonal beginning might succeed better than the usual collaboration poem to spark the reserved, reluctant older student. Students older than twelve might feel uncomfortable with anything that seems to them to be silly.

One kind of collaboration poem useful for young children based on a shared experience simply asks each child to supply an idea. For instance, you might use an apple. What does it look like to you? What does it taste like? What does it smell like? What does it feel like? How does it make you feel? You might want to accept volunteers only at first, but as the group warms up, try to encourage the shy ones to contribute. If you tape their responses, you can reproduce them later. However, in the beginning, immediacy is more successful. As they make their contributions, express pleasure and encouragement. Immediate visual recording of their lines gives importance and pleasure, even if they are too young to read. Collaboration poems go best if there is someone directing and someone taking dictation as words or lines are contributed. Don't let the experience continue too long. The younger the class, the sooner the collaboration poem is finished and it is time to do something else. The older elementary student can handle a more complex collaboration poem. A flower can be a useful shared inspiration. If the children are older and you are afraid that some of them, particularly the boys, may have learned to be prejudiced against flowers, use an interesting weed, leaves, or even blades of grass. If you can give one to each student, it is helpful. If silliness threatens, you can say that you are going to "study" this object, or perhaps that you are going to practice observing the way poets do.

As you begin the collaboration poem, it would be useful to make headings on the chalk board of the five senses. Ask the students to contribute words that express the sense of sight. If they contribute words that fit under the other senses, list them under the proper heading. Put down all the words. If two words contributed are very similar, put them together. Make lists under each heading. The students will probably start out with very general words like green, thin, smooth, or rough. Accept these, but begin to ask for more specific words. Exactly how does it look to you? Applaud vivid original contributions. They may begin to contribute phrases. When this begins, suggest that they all try for phrases instead of individual words. By this time you may need to move to another part of the chalk board or erase the lists.

You are ready to start keeping things for your first collaboration poem when the phrases start growing into lines. If no one tells how the topic makes him feel, you can suggest that they say things about the emotions evoked by the subject. Write down the contributed lines which you instinctively feel will go together to make an interesting poem. You are helping these students to see ideas take shape into a poem. With your comments on the special qualities of certain words, phrases, and lines, you are helping them sharpen their powers of observation, develop discrimination, and improve their taste and expression. This whole process must not take so long that it becomes tedious. After you have several lines written, you might ask for suggestions as to the best order in which to write them. With some groups it works to ask them to copy their poems. Some pupils will immediately ask if they may change theirs or add to it, or even write another one!

Sometimes you might need to ask for a volunteer to copy the poem for you so that you can have it reproduced and passed out, or mounted for display in the room. During this procedure, many of the students' misconceptions about poetry will be aired. Some will complain that it doesn't rhyme, and you can tell them that poems don't have to rhyme. Many will be amazed that this is called a poem, so you have an opportunity to discuss (for only a little while) what a poem really is.

An important value in this procedure is that you have written a poem so that everyone had a part in it and could see how it was done. Usually this dispels all the mysticism surrounding poetry writing and shows the students how to respond to objects in their lives through their senses. It is only one kind of poetry writing, of course, but because it is life-experience oriented, it is easy for most middle grade students, and it is a good place to start.

SILVER AND GOLD

Silver and gold is the thread that I knit with
If I slept in a room that was silver and gold
   I would feel like a king
Silver looks like a mirror
Silver looks like a glass
Silver looks like stars
Silver smells like a waterfall
Silver tastes like Listerine, toothpaste,
   and vinegar
Gold looks like squash
Gold looks like a hot burning light
   shining in darkness
Silver sounds like birds in wind, or chicken
   frying
Gold shines like the sun
Silver shines like snow.

Collaboration poem, *ages 10 and 11*

ABOUT SUMMER

I feel warm in the summer
The air feels good
The flowers smell good
When you go in swimming
The water feels good.

Sometime in your backyard a rabbit will jump
If you go to the beach, you might step on a jellyfish
And you would feel like you were shot by a BB gun
And if you build a sand castle too close to the ocean
The waves will knock it down
And the waves will knock you down.
In the summer I like to eat banana popsicles
I like to look in the mirror
Because I look good in the summer
And I like to listen to the summer night-time birds.

Collaboration poem, *age 6*

MOSTLY BLUE BOB

Bob Dylan sings blue out of breath
He is a pink pen of red ink
He is sad colors of purple, red, and blue
He is red because his heart is nice
He is purple-green like he is from the country
He sounds like blue eyes that grow in the dark.

Collaboration poem, *ages 10 and 11*
Written to Bob Dylan's music

I used to be a baby but now I am a six foot chalkboard
I used to eat baby food but now I eat steak
I used to be a bright emerald and now I have lost my sparkle

I used to be a sky but now I am a chair
I used to suck my thumb but now I bite my fingernails
I used to lock up dogs but now I have pets
I used to be a wart but now I'm smart.

Collaboration poem, *ages 8 and 9*

The Junk Poem

Provide students with one page or torn strips from the newspaper. Have them select lines (their junk) and combine them into poems. Be sure to get a variety from the newspaper of comic pages, sports pages, horoscopes, obituaries, ads, and weather reports. This exercise is especially stimulating and fun at the high school level, and can provide some vivid and startling combinations that may stretch imaginations.

The Concrete Poem

Poems that have their meanings reinforced by the arrangement of words on the page can be fun at any level if the teaching poet enjoys the frivolity and energy of this type of poem. The discussion might cover hieroglyphics, picture writing, codes, and Gestalt patterns and expand student attitudes toward the possibilities in language. Ideas for this sort of poem include: kite, light bulb, house, puzzle, sun, big dipper, altar, runaway, outside, jump, traffic, mailbox.

The Limerick

This familiar form is well suited to wit and lighthearted moods, but the attempt by young students often deteriorates into silliness and is sometimes destructive of expression since sense is frequently sacrificed to form in this exercise.

Cinquain (Take Five)

This form is especially useful with students who are insistent that they cannot write a poem at all. Give them this problem and they will be surprised at the poetic quality of their work.

Line 1. Noun
Line 2. Two adjectives that describe the noun
Line 3. Three verbs that tell what the noun does
Line 4. A phrase that tells something about the noun
Line 5. The noun again, or a synonym, or related word

Sky
Blue, cold
Moving, covering earth
Forever it is there
Space.

> Bill Jackson, *age 12*

Sand
Sparkling, white
Gleaming, spreading, flying
Moving any and everywhere.
Grains.

> Sherry Henderson, *age 12*

Mouse
Small, fast
Running for mouse hole
Never will catch one
Nuisance.

> Nolan Mills, *age 11*

            Seagull
         Alone, Together
     Soaring, Gliding, Floating,
  Drawn out wings leaving us behind
          White bird.

       Jim Wear, *age 15*

Haiku

The haiku is a Japanese form consisting of only three lines having 5, 7, 5 syllables, or 17 in all. Traditional Japanese haiku usually contained a word to suggest the season of the year, and thus is seasonal as well as being sensual—involving imagery and mood. Modern haiku is more concerned with everyday occurrences which evoke personal thoughts, feelings, and emotions. There are no requirements as to rhyme or rhythm and this form is easy and useful whenever the poet-teacher wishes to expose the students to discipline in language.

  This beautiful place
  Like the Garden of Eden
  Surrounds our bodies.

       CeCe Williamson, *age 12*

  Oh, colorful fish,
  how can you live in the cold
  water, when we can't?

       Hap Newell, *age 12*

  In the cool water
  The small ship stands deserted.
  Where is the owner?

       Caroline Scott, *age 12*

The man who is kind
Reaps happiness in life
And goes far in dreams.

Jones Oliver, *age 14*

5. Language as Therapy

When we work with language, we have a significant opportunity to teach the child discovery and to emphasize the good things in life. It is our responsibility to give encouragement to the positive attitudes which are natural to normal children, and one of the most important things an adult who works with children can do is to understand and respect the happiness in a child's life.

Destructive and negative attitudes are also normal and should be given expression. When problems exist in a child's life, language can become part of their solution. Verbalization is the best means of treatment in all psychotherapy. Language has been recognized as therapeutic since Apollo was imagined as god of both medicine and poetry, since Aristotle discussed catharsis of the emotions and Sophocles diagnosed the Oedipus complex.

Any exercises in talking or writing which focus on the language of feeling, which are directed toward freedom of expression and the release of creativity, may also result in the discovery of suppressed feelings. A sensitive response on the part of the parent or teacher can lead to constructive new self-awareness on the part of the young writer. If an encouraging start is given to writing, and an attentive listener is available, there is much to be learned beyond facility with language.

Because poetry is essentially the language of feeling, it is most often the writing of poetry that discharges fervent emotions, vents feelings that are usually repressed. The experience of writing poetry can be healing.

The reading and writing of poetry has been explored and praised by therapists working with deaf children, drug addicts, with retarded, violent, or disturbed children. Poetry as therapy has reached such children where all other attempts have failed. One of the methods used with cases of extreme behavior is to read poems about feelings, poems like Emily Dickinson's "I'm Nobody, Who Are You?" to youngsters with identity problems, or Robert Frost's poem about decision, "The Road Not Taken," to those who are indecisive and depressed, or poems about beauty to the catatonic. The result seems to be that the patient understands and identifies with another's need, a crucial step toward rehabilitation. Another method is to ask those who are emotionally isolated to write their own poems. The results are often encounters with emotions that the writer can deal with more easily once they are expressed on paper. There they are more removed, accessible, steady enough to deal with gradually. Anxieties and adversity expressed as poems can be examined in a way that is indirect and does not make a direct threat to the individual. Young patients in drug therapy seem more able to cope with their experience once they verbalize the feelings that led them into drugs and when they also have the emotional high of intense poetry as a substitute. Poetry as therapy has also been used in Veterans Hospitals and by medical doctors who praise its value as relief for ulcers, depression, and hypochondria.

Those of us who are parents or teachers will seldom see problems as critical as these, but we can learn much from the experiments in poetry therapy. All of us have known children in the school system who habitually refuse to conform, who are in a constant revolt against the status quo. These attitudes can and should be made constructive. The work of poets who protest violence, hypocrisy, indifference, and the ills of society give verification to the student's feelings and to the tradition of creative complaint. Anthologies of protest or individual poems by Kenneth Patchen, Lawrence Ferlinghetti, or Allen Ginsberg give reinforcement and direction to young people with similar concerns. An expression of grief and fear can be a catharsis and these topics might be suggested along with other topics so that the children always have an option and are not required to examine emotions that distress them. In poems like these, distress and monsters often become laughable and the sharing of sadness becomes a comfort.

The verbalization of anger and rage is also constructive. Expressed hostility provides a release and should not be disparaged when it occurs in student writing. Teachers and parents should always be aware of the power of language to uncover emotional flaws as well as to produce pleasurable communication. Common sense is necessary in reacting to children's expressions and when disturbances become evident in their writing we should get professional help to that child. With sensitivity, we can give much aid, but when the symptoms indicate need for more than listening and sharing, we should seek professional assistance in evaluating and helping the child.

HIGH

As you're floating around in the sky,
You wonder how you got high.
Was it grass, pills or a weird machine,
That put you on this psychedelic scene?
As you come down from the sky,
You wonder why that guy told you a lie.
"An ordinary pill," "No harm in it,"
But when you come down you're really sick.
Maybe it was worth seeing all those colors in the sky,
But you'll think twice before you give it another try.

Steve Jones, *age 13*

I'M JUST ME

I'm just me, you see,
Nobody can be like me, you see:
There is a key to me,
I'm just no good:
I'm so bad and different

      Jamie Glenn, *age* 10

NO KEYS

She peeks onward,
    Looking for a road;
A road to lead her to success . . .

But she finds no road.
She is lost, lost in an ugly world
    of discouraging thoughts,
        disappointing words.
Lost and locked, with no keys
    to freedom—imprisoned
        from all rays of happiness.

      Jane Freeman, *age* 17

A TALKED POEM

I'm Marty.
I like to beat up my little sister.
My big sister beats me up.
My mama whips me when I beat up my sister.
When they make me mad
I just start beating up on people.
The most important thing about me
    is I'm a boy.

I don't want nobody to think
   I'm a girl.

       Marty Daniels, *age 12*

HELLO TIPPY!

I wish I could bring back my little puppy dog,
So very much,
With all the power I got.
If I was a magician,
These are the words I would say,
"Abra Cadabra, with all the power
God and I have,
Please, please bring her back."
I pray with everything I've got.
Just bring her back.
I really want her back.

       Linda Street, *age 12*

GLASS

Glass is like ice
Glass can cut you like when you
get a divorce.
You can see through glass like
you can see through love.

       Tommy Bass, *age 10*

WONDER ABOUT, WORRY ABOUT

When I was young I never worried about anything,
but now that I am ten, things are different. I
worry about getting my science research in on
time and like now I'm worried about the science
fair.

I wonder what people would be like without eyes, noses, mouths, and ears. I also wonder more than anything if I will ever become what I want to be, a television actress. If I cannot do that I'll never be happy and satisfied with my life. I'm afraid of dying at an early age and I'm afraid of snakes. I am afraid of forest fires and my father when he gets mad. I am afraid of drug addicts and pushers and most of all of drugs themselves. I am afraid of many animals becoming extinct and I worry about my parents and my sister dying.

I used to be afraid that I would be sucked down with the water through the drain in the bathtub and afraid that I would flush myself down the toilet. But now I am afraid of many people and things that I never thought of when I was five or six. I am afraid of 40 or 50 years from now when the world will die. I worry about pollution and population, sickness and death and I am afraid of the ever-changing earth.

I am afraid of the dark. I am most afraid of the dark when I am outside and I have to pass alleys or corners. I am afraid somebody will be there and I will be stolen or killed.

I am afraid of my mother and so is my daddy. He is a very smart man.

I am afraid of going into a place for the first time if I don't know anybody.

I am afraid if I do not get good grades.

Seven children, *ages 10, 11, and 12*

THE ALTERNATIVE

I had the key to every door in the corridor
I could open any door I wanted to
I could open one door
I could open all the doors
I could keep them all locked
It was up to me to decide.

I had heard that it was cold
Behind some of those doors
But I didn't know if that was true.
I had heard that there was a monster
Behind one door
But I knew that wasn't true.
I looked through most of the key holes
To make sure.

Finally one day I unlocked my first door.
I didn't open it very fast
But I soon discovered that it was just a closet
With nothing inside
But a bucketful of tangerines and eggs
And, pretty soon, it became very interesting
To imagine my bare feet
Crushing tangerines and eggs.

So I threw away the keys
And took off my shoes.

Stuart Troutman, *age 18*

6. Evaluation of Children's Writing

Creativity develops children. Any creative writing exercise should be seen as a process more important than the product. The results of a child's attempt to express himself in written language should be judged in relationship to the child who produced the work. Does this particular piece show growth in imagination and freedom of expression for this particular child?

Don't expect children to write literature. The literary quality of children's writing is immaterial to the success of their creative expression. The "best" written work of children is not that which most closely resembles adult style and standards but is that which best expresses the mind and life of the child. The criteria for evaluation should always be the child and childhood—not adult literary standards.

Try to approach the child's writing with these attitudes: "The child is speaking. I will let him speak." Watch progressive written exercises and see if the child is growing in ability to observe. Is he making more acute and critical observations? Has he perceived something he did not see before? Has he perceived it in an original way? Is he expressing an original thought in his own language and not just parroting what someone else has said to him or repeating something he has read?

The most important thing to do is to listen and to accept. When evaluating the children's work to them, the thing they need most to hear is that you are listening, so whatever you say, let it mean, "I hear you." If you do listen, the children will keep on talking and writing, and you will keep the avenues open for continued communication. If you make favorable comments on specific literary aspects of the writing such as perceptions and style, the literary quality of the writing will gradually improve. Interest in the accurate use of the mechanics of English will grow as the child comes to value skill in communication.

7. Encouragement of Creative Writing

Creative writing is good for everyone. It broadens perceptions and appreciation. It is a means of self-discovery. It can be great fun. If you are just beginning to encourage creative expression in children, try to choose topics for writing that suit their maturity and capture their interest. Try to find a topic that also appeals to you since your enthusiasm is important to the success of young writers.

The use of primary experience as a motivation for writing is an effective means for developing awareness. Give the children objects that they can touch, smell, see, or taste. An experience they share increases attention span and gives more equal opportunity for expression to any child who may be culturally deprived.

Talk a little before writing begins. Sharing ideas is stimulating. But do not talk too long for if too much is said, there won't be enough left to write. If you are in a classroom where some students are slow to begin, you might move around the room to give individual encouragement. Help the child think of something he knows about and can express.

Prose writing has been emphasized more but you will probably find that poetry writing is easier for children. In the writing of poems it is possible for the child to say whatever he wants to say however he wants to say it. No preset forms or mechanics are required. The encouragement that poetry gives to an expression of feelings, the freedom to be personal and original are a delight to most children. They love to take complete command of their language with the assurance that they can make no mistakes.

Creative writing sessions are not proper times for demanding accurate English mechanics. Such emphasis inhibits free expression. Assure students that punctuation, spelling, and handwriting are not as important as getting down what they think and feel. If the story, poem, or play is to be published or otherwise put on display, there will be time to go back and make any desired corrections later. Do not even discuss form during the creative sessions. Such teaching should be entirely disassociated from the time of writing. Attention to form may detract from expression of meaning. Children will let you know when they are ready to use specific forms. Often they will discover their own as they develop their personal writing style.

Children who have lacked opportunities to exercise their imaginations and express themselves creatively will find that imaginative and free use of language becomes increasingly difficult as they grow older. This failure to derive personal meaning and satisfaction in the use of language inhibits motivation and success in all areas of study. Encourage children's expression by accepting everything they say and leading them slowly to make more specific and original descriptions, comparisons, and contrasts. Help them learn to give explanations, share and interpret ideas, understand relationships, and perceive absurdities. Teach them to identify causes and effects and distinguish these from happenings that occur coincidentally without being related except in time. Help them to recognize categories, classify objects and events, and make valid judgments about them; recognize problems and learn how to work toward solutions; learn the process of decision-making, and recognize varying points of view. Love and respect for language, growth in the skill of using it fluently, creatively, and accurately enables children to think more clearly and logically. Enjoyment of the creative use of language is a prerequisite to the highest development of mature personal integrity, and the willingness to assume responsibility for what is said and for its consequences.